A MASSACRE AVERTED

A Massacre Averted

An Armenian Town, an American Nurse, and the Turkish Army They Resisted

THE MEMOIRS OF MARY WATSON SUPER

Edited and Introduced by
NANCY KLANCHER

 Markus Wiener Publishers
Princeton

For information, write to
Markus Wiener Publishers
231 Nassau Street, Princeton, NJ 08542
www.markuswiener.com

Library of Congress Cataloging-in-Publication Data

Super, Mary, d. 1965.
    A massacre averted : an Armenian town, an American nurse, and the Turkish army they resisted / edited and introduced by Nancy Klancher.
    p. cm.
    Including bibliographical references.
    ISBN 978-1-55876-532-0 (hardcover : acid-free paper)
    ISBN 978-1-55876-533-7 (pbk. : acid-free paper)
    1. Super, Mary, d. 1965. 2. Turkey—History—Revolution, 1918-1923—Personal narratives, American. 3. Hacin (Turkey)—History—Siege, 1920.
4. Nurses—United States—Biography. 5. Armenians—Turkey—Hacin—History—20th century. 6. Hacin (Turkey)—Ethnic relations—History—20th century. 7. Turkey—History—Revolution, 1918-1923—Social aspects. 8. Relief work—Turkey—Hacin—History—20th century. 9. Turkey—History—Revolution, 1918-1923—Medical care. 10. Turkey—History—Revolution, 1918-1923—Sources. I. Klancher, Nancy. II. Title.
    DR589S85 2010
    956.1'023—dc22
    [B]
    2010039291

Markus Wiener Publishers books are printed in the United States of America on acid-free paper and meet the guidelines for permanence and durability of the Committee on Production Guidelines for Book Longevity of the Council on Library Resources.

CONTENTS

ACKNOWLEDGMENTS

I wish to express my thanks for the help and encouragement of Ruth Thomasian of Project SAVE; Ted Goldsborough of the Lower Merion Historical Society; the research assistants, especially Sally Kuisel, at the National Archives and Records Administration who sent me documents on the Hadjin relief workers; Mohammed Bamyeh at the University of Pittsburgh; Dale Allison at the Pittsburgh Theological Seminary; and Shant Mardirossian of the Near East Foundation. I wish also to thank my daughters, Sophie and Maya, for their daily offerings of righteous indignation, questions, and humor on all manner of subjects, including these memoirs.

In all the countries around the Eastern Mediterranean and along the shores of the Black Sea, the names "American Near East Relief" and "American Committee" are held in affectionate regard. Whoever journeys there under these names is recognized as a friend. To the millions of peoples in all those countries our country was the Good Samaritan that did not pass them by but bound up their wounds and poured into their troubled lives the consoling oil of sympathy and healing . . .

The work of the Committee has demonstrated practical Christianity without sectarianism, and without ecclesiastical form, recognizing the rights of each and all to their ancestral faith, while expressing religion in terms of sacrifice and service that others might live and be benefited. Its creed was the Golden Rule and its ritual the devotion of life and treasure to the healing of wounds caused by war.

Calvin Coolidge, introduction to
The Story of Near East Relief (1915-1930):
An Interpretation, by James L. Barton
(New York: Macmillan, 1930), ix.

Introduction

My first connection to the author of the memoirs in this volume was personal. Mary Super was a close friend of my grandmother and a familiar presence at family gatherings during my early childhood. She was a midwife and nurse and delivered my father and his four brothers. In 2001, I found her memoirs in my grandmother's belongings and discovered that Mary had been a Red Cross Nurse in the city of Hadjin, in the Taurus Mountains, Cilicia (south and center of present-day Turkey), in 1920, precisely when Turkish and Kurdish Kemalists had laid siege to the small mountain town for two months. Mary's memoirs tell the story of her work in Cilicia before and during the siege. She arrived in January 1919 and by April 1920 she and her fellow relief workers found themselves in the middle of the Turkish Nationalist war of independence. Among other acts of bravery, the relief workers successfully protected and kept alive approximately 300 Armenian orphans for the duration of the siege. In doing so, they became active participants in what turned out to be a sustained yet tenuous, psychologically complex negotiation between themselves, the Armenians living in Hadjin, and a diverse coalition of Nationalist soldiers. This story of intercultural and interreligious encounter is the topic of Mary's memoirs.

On March 31, 1920, Turkish Nationalist soldiers surrounded the city of Hadjin and its largely Armenian population for approximately two months. Two Canadian and four American relief workers (including Mary) were occupying a compound on an escarpment east of the town. They had come a little over a year before to support the painful repa-

1

triation of Armenians in Hadjin and surrounding villages, that is, to help the survivors of the government's mass deportations of Armenians in 1915 and 1916. During the deportations countless Armenian lives had been lost. By 1919-1920, the poverty and illness of the surviving population returning home and the needs of thousands of displaced and orphaned children were dire.

The Turkish Nationalists, or Kemalists, took their name from their leader, Mustafa Kemal Ataturk, who was to become the founder of the current Westernized, secularized Republic of Turkey. Ataturk had been an Ottoman field commander during World War I. When the armistice was signed, he began maneuvering to combat all foreign occupation of his Turkish homeland, beginning in Cilicia, and to establish Turkish national independence. He requested the position of inspector general of the Third and Ninth Armies in Anatolia so that he could quietly build a national revolutionary army while the British and French were arguing about how to divide up the spoils of World War I.[1]

And so, in April 1920, Mary Super and her fellow relief workers found themselves in the middle of a war zone, not a war zone of inhuman remote-control shock and awe, but one of close-range human interactions, hostility and negotiation, distrust and curiosity. The 1920 siege of Hadjin, as narrated in Mary's memoirs, required strategic restraint and control on the part of all who found themselves there. This restraint enabled a heightened intercultural exchange with high stakes that, in turn, made possible a suspension of wholesale massacre, if not serious violence. Against all odds, this limbo lasted several months as Armenians, Turks, Kurds, Americans, Canadians, Muslims, and Christians confronted one another.

Three sets of memoirs that tell the story of the siege of Hadjin, written by three of the Western women who were there, survive. Two were published within a few years of the siege. In 1922, *At the Mercy of Turkish Brigands: A True Story* appeared, written by Blanche Remington Eby, wife of the Canadian Mennonite missionary D. C. Eby, both of whom were in the compound with Mary Super during the siege.[2]

---

1. Stanley Elphinstone Kerr, *The Lions of Marash: Personal Experiences with American Near East Relief, 1919-1922* (New York: State University of New York, 1973), 65.

2. Blanche Remington Eby, *At the Mercy of Turkish Brigands: A True Story* (New Carlisle, Ohio: Bethel Publishing Co., 1922).

This first account, which we will turn to only for corroborating or elaborative detail, is a pious, romance-inflected narrative, characterized by a sometimes sentimental, sometimes titillated orientalist sensibility.

In 1924, Alice Keep Clark, an American relief worker also in the compound and working closely with Mary Super throughout her time in Hadjin, published her *Letters From Cilicia*, which featured letters she had written home to her family and a journal in epistolary form that she kept for the duration of the siege, even after mail and telegram services had been cut off.[3] Alice's letters reveal an elite, literate, well-traveled, and privileged American woman.[4] Her observations evolved from aloof travelogue-like critiques of the aesthetic and intellectual novelties that Cilicia afforded to her to alert analysis of historical and political developments and deep regret at the loss of human dignity and life that escalated around her. Alice's letters are useful for their characterization of Mary and of others who interacted during the siege.

Reverend and Blanche Eby   Alice Clark (from *Letters*)
(from *At the Mercy*)

---

3. Alice Keep Clark, *Letters from Cilicia* (Chicago: A. D. Weinthrop & Co., 1924).

4. The social and economic status of Alice's family is reflected in the many telegrams and letters sent to the State Department, the U.S. Secretary of State, and various senators by Alice's brother and father, the latter of whom owned a division of American Stove Company in Chicago.

In contrast, Mary Super's memoirs, unpublished until now, read sometimes like diary entries, sometimes like letters, and sometimes like the field notes of an anthropologist. They are the observations of a pragmatist who was scientifically minded, understated, and culturally inquisitive. Though Mary embodies her time and her religion just like the others, she is at once more reserved, more curious, and more analytical in her approach to understanding the people and interactions around her. Perhaps not unrelated to her openness in this regard is Mary's inclusion in her memoirs of an episode that is not treated in detail in the other two sets of memoirs. She recounts a period during which the Armenians of Hadjin imprisoned and persecuted their Turkish neighbors. Mary was extremely aware of, and sensitive to, the interactions among all the different groups that surrounded her before and during the siege, though she does not appear to have had much prior knowledge about the culture and context into which she ventured.

The History behind the Memoirs:
Cultural and Religious Identities in a Dying Ottomanism

The very human interactions across religion, class, gender, and nationality that punctuate Mary Super's memoirs had a history.[5] In particular, they may be understood as embodying the continual shifts and reversals in cultural identities and in evolving discourses of intercultural relations that characterized the turn of the century in Ottoman Turkey.[6] The experiences in the memoirs reflect a long history of ethnic loyalties, mutual interests and hostilities, interference by other countries, and a dynasty that had for hundreds of years actively manipulated the terms

---

5. This short account of the history and politics that preceded the siege of Hadjin reflects my own selective emphases as a Religious Studies scholar interested in religious identity and interreligious conflict. It has been culled from standard histories, missionary accounts, newspaper articles, and the memoirs of the siege itself, some of which are included in the appendixes and selected bibliography. The basic history is here but organized primarily to provide a frame for the interactions and (mis)understandings across ethnic and religious difference in the memoirs.

6. For more on the history covered in the next three pages, cf. Vahakn N. Dadrian, *The History of the Armenian Genocide: Ethnic Conflict from the Balkans to Anatolia to the Caucasus* (New York: Berghahn Books, 1995), esp. 99-104; Hovannisian, Richard G., ed., *The Armenian Genocide: History, Politics, Ethics* (New York: Palgrave Macmillan, 1992), esp. Stephan H. Astourian, 53-79; and Erik J. Zürcher, *Turkey: A Modern History* (New York: I. B. Tauris & Co., Ltd., 1993).

by which its subjects identified themselves: imperial (Ottoman), national (Turkish, Greek, Armenian), religious (Muslim, Christian), and ethnic (Turkish, Arab, Armenian, Kurdish, Greek, Jewish).

The successive governing forces in Turkey from the beginning of the nineteenth century through World War I all leveraged in one way or another the question of identity.[7] The progressive *Tanzimat* reforms of 1839-1876 had called for a universal or shared Ottoman identity, democratic constitutionalism, Westernized systems of government, and equal rights for all Ottoman citizens, Muslim and non-Muslim. In the 1860s and 1870s, a group of young intellectuals, the Young Ottomans, tried to synthesize the complex multinational history they inherited by balancing Western democratic ideals with Islamic foundations, promoting reliance on Islamic cultural and political roots *and* advocating an equal coalition of diverse Ottoman patriots. In contrast, Sultan Abdulhamid II, who succeeded them, forcefully promoted a pan-Islamic state. Then, again, Ottoman tolerance seemed to be returning with the Young Turk Revolution of 1908-1913. The Young Turks formed an alliance comprising diverse partners and initially sought a diverse multiethnic empire. The Young Turk alliance included Ottoman liberals, who advocated for a multinational Ottoman state; Armenian *Dashnaktsutiun* (the Dashnaks), who advocated for Armenian autonomy within the Ottoman Empire; and the army officers of the *Ittihad ve Terakki*, or Committee of Union and Progress (CUP).

During the years between the initial 1908 revolt of the Young Turks and 1913, however, the CUP leaders, Enver, Talat, and Jamal Pashas, relentlessly worked to acquire sole control of the government, and by the 1909 countercoup in Istanbul, they too were challenged, by their former allies, the Ottoman Liberals, for betraying their original coalition politics, and also by common soldiers and theology students who opposed them as too modernizing, too Europeanized, not Islamic enough. All of these examples illustrate how politically expedient

---

7. For just one example, consider Stephan Astourian's description (using Habermas's notion of *habitus*) of the impact of the *Tanzimat* reforms: "A traditional society is based on an institutional framework which 'consists of norms that guide symbolic interaction.' The impact of the *Tanzimat* on such a traditional society and on Armeno-Turkish relations was radical, for it undermined centuries-old social norms and institutions, altered reciprocal expectations about behavior among Armenians and Turks, and slowly reshaped their role-in-internalization" (in Hovannisian, *The Armenian Genocide*, 57.)

established discourses of identity were. The competing claims of Ottoman, Islamic, and Turkish identity, and of the nationalist movements in the Balkans, Armenia, and Macedonia, placed extraordinary pressure on what had been the CUP leaders' initial commitment to a unified Ottoman identity.

But, by all accounts, minority groups, especially the Armenians, had no illusions about such ideals in any case. Indeed, the history of the Armenians makes a travesty of the ideals of Ottoman universalism. It exposes the links between national and religious identities, on the one hand, and the solidifying of power, leveraging of popular support, and justifying of violence against ethnic minorities, on the other.

For the Armenians had consistently been the victims of Ottoman fears about their independence and loyalties, and of violent attempts to maintain the borders of the empire by retaining control of the Armenian provinces in eastern Anatolia. This history directly contributed to ethnic and racial animosities, evident in the internationally reported Hamidian massacres of 1894-1896. Furthermore, whatever the political justifications for these conflicts were, according to Western relief workers in the area at the time, they were also expressly carried out in religious terms in the name of religious survival—defending the Islamic faith against Christian incursions.[8]

Later, during the deportations of 1915-1916, religious justifications for continued opposition and violence intensified on *all* sides. The rhetoric of American politicians and philanthropists who called for solidarity among Christians in every land is epitomized in a special message from President Woodrow Wilson to Congress on May 24, 1920, in which he refers to the American people as "the greatest of the Christian peoples," and describes American concern for the Armenians as "sprung from untainted consciences, pure Christian faith and an earnest desire to see Christian people everywhere succored in their time of suffering and lifted up from their abject subjection . . ."[9] This potent

---

8. Kerr, *Lions of Marash*, 34. [See also Appendix B.2.]

9. *A Compilation of the Messages and Papers of the Presidents: Prepared Under the Direction of the Joint Committee on Printing of the House and Senate, Pursuant to an Act of the Fifty-Second Congress of the United States (With Additions and Encyclopedic Index by Private Enterprise), Volume XVIII* (New York: Bureau of National Literature, Inc.). Reproduced in *The Armenian Genocide and America's Outcry: A Compilation of U.S. Documents 1890-1923* (Washington D.C.: Armenian Assembly of America, 1985), 8853. [Appendix A.4.]

amalgamation of Christian solidarity and Western paternalism carries within it the rationale for imperialist opportunism and the barely veiled cultural chauvinism that undergird American civil religion. On the other side, however, newspaper reports in the *Washington Post* of the crucifying and burning alive of "native Christian preachers"—that is, Syrian Nestorians and Armenians—in the city of Urumiah just five years earlier, on April 29, 1915, attest to the religious framing and articulation of Kurdish and Turkish violence as well.[10]

At the same time, there was no dearth of rationales leveraged to justify violence against Armenians. In 1909, when the theology students and soldiers rose up against CUP constitutionalism, the Armenians in Adana suffered collateral violence, accused of having supported the restoration of the constitution.[11] But the absolute nadir in the history of the Armenian people was their forced deportation during World War I into the Syrian desert. Their path across the Cilician plain, from Aleppo to Der Zor, and as far east as Mosul in Iraq resulted in the death of countless Armenians.

In the context of World War I and the external threats on the eastern front, some within the CUP government had begun to argue that the agitating of Armenian nationalist organizations was evidence of their collaboration with the Russian enemy.[12] And so, in early 1915, the deportation of Armenians began.

We find this forced march towards the Syrian desert described in the memoirs of Blanche Eby in a chapter entitled "The Trail of Death." Blanche recounts the personal stories of survivors she knew and with whom she spoke, and they are harrowing and detailed. She also transmits reports of the presence of CUP soldiers alongside local bands of Kurdish "brigands,"[13] all of whom assaulted, robbed, and tortured Armenians as they marched, and kidnapped and raped Armenian girls and women. One of Blanche's eyewitnesses, whom she calls "Menas Effendi," and who appears in all three women's memoirs as steward for the Hadjin mission station both before and after the exile, lists the presence of Turks, Kurds, Arabs, and Circassians among the "Moslem

---

10. *Washington Post*, "Crucified by Turks," April 29, 1915. [Appendix B.2.]
11. Dadrian, *History of the Armenian Genocide*, 181-84.
12. See Appendixes C.1, C.2, C.3, and C.4.
13. Eby, *At the Mercy*, 27 ff. [Appendix E.2.]

soldiers" policing and torturing the deportees en route.[14] Diseases, especially typhus, dysentery, and cholera, also killed many,[15] in addition to starvation, exposure, violence, and execution.

Mary's memoirs begin in January 1919. This is the year the survivors of the deportations returned home under the protection of French soldiers: "The French governor supervised the return of one hundred twenty thousand of the exiles to their homes in Cilicia, repopulating cities as far away as Marash, Zeitun, Aintab, and Hadjin."[16]

E. Stanley Kerr, a medical missionary who was living and working in Marash before the Nationalists attacked in January 1920, reports that earlier, before the end of the war, Near East Relief (NER) workers were unable to enter Ottoman territories to provide aid. Nonetheless, according to Kerr, due to the advocacy of Ambassador Henry Morgenthau and the efforts of the American Committee for Armenian and Syrian Relief (ACASR), hundreds of thousands of dollars had already been sent. Because the CUP leaders were aware of this flow of money and resented American interference, its distribution was often accomplished covertly or indirectly. During the deportations and exile, Kerr tells us, monies were funneled through Morgenthau to German missionaries and Armenian pastors who "followed the caravans of deportees in order to give what help was possible."[17]

For the plight of the Armenians was internationally reported in Western newspapers. Campaigns to raise money, indignation, and political resolve were broadly orchestrated.[18] Even a cursory glance at the political cartoons that appeared in the Western press, circa 1919-1920, demonstrates awareness among the general population of the conflicts and atrocities that were under way.[19] American response to the events of 1915-1919 was philanthropic; the goal was humanitarian aid and not political or military intervention. Many cartoons depict a female Armenia begging for more substantial protection from an evasive male United States.

---

14. Eby, *At the Mercy,* 34.
15. Eby, *At the Mercy,* 42.
16. Kerr, *Lions of Marash,* 36.
17. Kerr, *Lions of Marash,* 29. [See also Appendix B.4.]
18. See Appendix B in its entirety.
19. Italian, French, German, British, and American cartoonists reflected full awareness of the massacres and caricatured the Western powers as pompous, passive, and/or indifferent in the face of need and atrocity. [Appendix B.9.]

The mobilization of humanitarian support was intensive and broad-based. With the sanction of the highest levels of government, from Woodrow Wilson to the American Board of Commissioners for Foreign Missions, the American Committee for Armenian and Syrian Relief (which was to incorporate as the Near East Relief, or NER, in 1919) raised the funds that were funneled through the American Embassy in Constantinople during and following the deportations.[20] The Committee conducted this massive fundraising effort on many fronts: letters and articles in local newspapers; cablegrams in the local press; posters in train stations, hotels, and streetcars and on public bulletin boards; announcements and leaflets in church programs and Sunday school drives; NER advertising space donated by businesses; relief funds through local papers; booksellers and public libraries featuring NER posters; public meetings and networking within women's organizations; leaflets in public places; door-to-door fundraising; and even pamphlets distributed in public schools that featured stories of children in the Near East who had experienced starvation and worse.[21]

Mary's Memoirs

This context, this social tableau of public outcry and calls for assistance, may explain, at least in part, Mary Super's extraordinary decision to pick up and travel to the mountains of Cilicia to provide medical care to Armenian refugees. It may also provide some insight into what her goals and reasoning might have been. The mobilization of Christian American humanitarianism was heavily moralistic, chauvinistic, and rhetorically constructed out of ideals of Christian compassion, *caritas*, and self-sacrifice. Mary's narrative voice in the memoirs emerges out of this discursive frame; it affects Mary's representation of others radically different from herself and how she judges their actions and words.

---

20. Cf. Donald E. Miller and Lorna Touryan Miller, *Survivors: An Oral History of the Armenian Genocide* (Berkeley and Los Angeles: University of California Press, 1993), 120-21, and Joseph L. Grabill, *Protestant Diplomacy and the Near East: Missionary Influence on American Policy, 1810-1927* (Minneapolis: University of Minnesota Press, 1971), 70 ff. [See also Appendix A.]

21. Mustafa Aydin and Cagri Erhan, eds., *Turkish-American Relations: Past, Present, and Future* (London: Routledge, 2004), 42-44. Aydin and Erhan provide this exhaustive list of the ACASR outreach to the American public.

Mary was a single woman, thirty-seven years of age, when she left for Cilicia. She was born and lived all of her life on her family's homestead in Narberth, Pennsylvania, in the company of many cousins, uncles, and aunts, the majority of whom lived out their lives as single and pious Christians. The homestead directly abutted the Philadelphia and Columbia Railroad and sported a wheelwright and blacksmith shop, probably run by the Super family, who had most likely been on that land from the 1850s on. The blacksmith shop was demolished circa 1970. There was a spring, the source of Indian Springs Creek, on the property, and some older Narberth residents remember a swimming pool on the Super land.[22] It is not clear where Mary received her nurse's training, but she identifies herself as a Red Cross Nurse on her passport application, and after her return from Cilicia she is listed in census reports, and in her obituary, as a nurse.

Mary was private, unemotional, old-fashioned, and plain in dress.[23] Outside of the events narrated in her memoirs, she had a quiet life and in 1965 was buried in a local Lutheran cemetery. Her obituary does not mention her time in Cilicia; indeed, it contains little information about her: "Miss Super, a practical nurse, was born in the family home. She was known for her helpfulness to others."[24] She is, however, listed in the official tribute to Near East Relief workers, along with Alice Clark, Edith Cold, and others who appear in the memoirs. The tribute was published by the Near East Relief itself in 1924 and was entitled *Teamwork: A Tribute and an Appeal*.[25]

Mary's memoirs, however, were anything but uneventful, and her articulate, thoughtful, and sometimes complex representations of what was happening around her complicate any one-dimensional portrait of her as quiet and private. In the uneasy tension in the memoirs between Mary's representations of personal experience and her accounts of others, we see a combination of "objective" generalizations, personal

---

22. Ted Goldsborough, Lower Merion Historical Society, personal correspondence, May 2001.
23. This personal information about Mary comes from my family members and from my own recollections.
24. Obituary for Mary Super, *Main Line Chronicle*, Ardmore, PA, July 22, 1965.
25. Charles V. Vickrey, *Teamwork: A Tribute and an Appeal*, ed. Mabell S. C. Smith (New York: Near East Relief National Headquarters Publication, 1924). [See Appendix F.2.]

value judgments, proverbs and sayings, patronizing humor, and essentializing acts of defining the Turks or "Moselems" within their past cultural and political history. Mary's scientific voice is dominant, yet a gentler, gender-inflected voice is also sometimes heard.[26] She articulates both her experiences and her observations within the terms of a variety of discourses—of religion, scientific inquiry, conventional femininity, and Christian humility.[27]

The notion of contending discursive conventions works well with Mary's memoirs, for Mary's voice fluctuates. She is frank and forceful when in her narrative she explains or passes judgment on the actions of others, including Westerners (adopting a kind of American Christian moral paternalism), and yet is remarkably reticent and unassuming about her own actions and hard work (exhibiting conventional Christian and female self-effacement and humility). The fact that she served in the capacity of a frontline combat medic during the last weeks of the siege is scarcely registered in her narrative, she so de-emphasizes her role. However, if one compares it with Blanche's descriptions of what Mary did, it is quite clear that she was at the center of traumatic combat experiences. For instance, below is Mary's account of her treatment of an Armenian soldier with a severed artery during the final violent takeover of the compound:

> Our last patient was a man with his radical artery severed. Nothing was left but a few horse sutures which were absolutely useless. I applied a two hemostal that I fortunately had carried into our closet and bandaged up the arm, keeping him a short time until we were sure the flow had ceased. We sent him to the druggist in the town for we could not keep him.

---

26. Consider, for example, her pleasure at sharing Christmas morning with the older girls at the orphanage: ". . . and on Christmas morning at five o'clock I heard a commotion at my room door. Very shortly after this they began singing the Christmas carols. After they had finished, fifteen young girls came around to the alcove, where my bed was standing, to wish me 'A Merry Christmas' and what a sight it was, each holding a lighted candle. Don't you think you would have enjoyed such a Christmas morning?"

27. Markers of class are absent, especially when compared with Alice Clark's palpably class-inflected impressions.

Compare this with Blanche's rendering of the treating of this same wounded Armenian:

> The Doctor Lady's trembling but skillful fingers sewed up wounds, while the Other One and the Married One assisted her.[28] . . . Just at dusk, when the Armenians who had planned a retreat were leaving, a soldier came down with a wounded wrist. Wide open, the severed artery was spouting a stream of bright red blood. . . . The man was rapidly bleeding to death. The Doctor Lady, fortunately, was able to produce a pair of artery clamps, and with these she deftly caught the ends of the artery . . . while she tied the artery with a piece of gut string. Unfortunately it was not fine enough; . . . as soon as the clamps were removed the artery burst forth afresh. The man had already lost a great quantity of blood, and his face was growing whiter. . . . The Doctor Lady tied the artery a second time with the same result. The blood spurted over her and her assistants, and the cellar steps had become so slippery they could scarcely stand on them . . .[29]

Mary's minimalism suggests a quick medical intervention; it shares nothing of her emotional response to the events, other than a spare, "This was rather difficult, for most of our supplies had been carried into town." In contrast, Blanche tells us that "Meudir Effendi [her husband, Mr. Eby] spoke a few encouraging words to the Doctor Lady, who was growing panicky," and just a few lines later, "The Doctor Lady was on the verge of collapse."[30]

Alice Clark's letters also attest to Mary's unrelenting work and her

---

28. One of the oddest aspects of Blanche's memoirs is her use of the names that *the Turkish Nationalist soldiers* gave to her and her fellow relief workers. Throughout the full narrative, she never refers to anyone except with these names, ostensibly representing the Westerners through the eyes of the Turks. So, Mary is called "the Doctor Lady"; Blanche, "the Married One"; Alice Clark, "The Tall One"; and Edith Cold, "The Little Lady." "The Other One" was Miss Brademons. Is her use of these names some sort of patronizing joke, an indication of how little the Turks understood who they were dealing with? Or, is it an act of emotional distancing: "That could not have been me who went through such things. It must have been 'the Married One'"?

29. Eby, *At the Mercy*, 230.

30. Eby, *At the Mercy*, 231.

almost frantic response to the human need and suffering she saw around her. Interestingly, Alice's comments, particularly in the early stages of her letter writing, sound almost annoyed, holding Mary (or perhaps the suffering with which Mary so relentlessly engaged) at arm's length: "Miss Super is working too hard. This morning, she went down to the city before five o'clock to see a woman who has malaria. We are urging her to give up outside calls for she will be ill herself before she knows it. She is absolutely absorbed in her profession and thinks of nothing else."[31] A little later, there are signs that Mary is wearing herself down: "Miss Super has been working terribly hard and she has given out for a day or two—she hopes to be up tomorrow. I keep remarkably well, hardly ever a headache."[32] As time goes on, however, Alice's appreciation for Mary grows: "Miss Super is indefatigable. She is devoted to the children and is a clever and ingenious nurse."[33]

And in the end, even Alice seems to have understood that, through healing Turks, Kurds, and Armenians, Mary had forged bonds that may have been a decisive factor in the holding off of violence during the siege. Throughout the diary, Mary describes herself meeting Turks, Armenians, commanders, and villagers at the same small valley gate where they would come with medical ailments, and she would administer medical care to them all together. She states outright the pragmatic reasons for this: "The Near East Relief never turned anyone away, feeling that this way we could protect the Armenians by being on friendly terms with the Turks." As Alice acknowledges about a month before the end, "Miss Super's work has been of great value to the compound for the Turks constantly come asking for her services."[34]

Meanwhile, Mary's interests are not in self-disclosure or self-analysis. Instead, she is turned outward to the world surrounding her. She recounts customs, cultural and seasonal observances, folk expressions both Armenian and Turkish, etiquette, diet, attitudes towards medicine, and the ways that the Armenians make gunpowder during the siege. She describes the stamping of grapes and their distillation into syrup in September, and the nighttime bonfires in February that symbolized

---

31. Clark, *Letters*, 50.
32. Clark, *Letters*, 88.
33. Clark, *Letters*, 95.
34. Clark, *Letters*, 168.

the "burning of winter," with children jumping and running in the fire-light and seeds being planted the next day. She is fond of the orphans under her care, but in an unsentimental, appreciative way.

Mary is interested in the relationship between the Turks and Arme-nians and recounts the distrust, repentance, mistakes, rage, and faith she sees in each group. The memoirs contain reported speech, and so represent a recuperation of sorts—however mediated by Mary's nar-rative—of the rarely heard voices of colonized Turks, Armenian vic-tims of genocide, and American Christian missionaries and relief workers from this period. But Mary's memoirs offer us more than the recuperation of "lost voices." The interactions and exchanges that are narrated allow us to ask critical questions. How do the groups appear to have understood each other? How do long-established discourses of nation, ethnicity, and religion surface in these exchanges? In the middle of a nationalist revolution, is the old ideal of Ottoman universalism ap-parent or residual anywhere? Does Mary as a Westerner perceive any of this, and how?

Universalist Claims, Intercultural Concessions

What did Mary understand about the different people among whom she found herself? Mary's accounts of the Armenians with whom she worked and to whom she provided medical care reveal two basic pre-occupations: the first, with the sufferings that they had endured; the second, with their Christianity. Throughout the memoirs, she registers the past victimization and residual distrust and anxiety she sees in the Armenians residing in Hadjin and in the children in the orphanage. Thus, Mary explains the repeated Armenian refusal to engage in nego-tiation or allow the Turkish Nationalists into their city as the direct re-sult of a history of Turkish betrayal and violence against them: "The Turks promised the Armenians protection if they would only remove the [French] flag and let the nationalists come through Hadjin un-harmed. But the Armenians refused to do this because from past expe-rience they had learned not to trust the Turks and one could not blame them for doing so."

Mary's account of the Armenian imprisonment and persecution of Turkish men in Hadjin, as the rumors of the Nationalists' approach intensified, is a particularly complex instance of this apologetic strain. Both Alice Clark and Blanche Eby mention this episode, but only very briefly. Blanche notes that the Armenians imprisoned all the Turks in the city. She describes how men were "gathered up" (both Turks and Kurds), and taken to prison "as a precautionary measure." One gets a sense that this was done precipitously: "Tools lay where the men had dropped them, and the work remained half finished."[35] Alice Clark's account is even more perfunctory. Indeed, she does not mention the imprisonment at all but indirectly argues against the French having given arms to the Armenians: "It is a policy which seems to us most unwise, for the Armenians, smarting from past cruelty and injustice, are certain to take it out on the Turks when the opportunity offers."[36] That she is thinking of this episode is apparent only from her next remark that the Turkish mayor had been removed and replaced by an Armenian, which was in fact accomplished shortly after the imprisonments.

There may be a mundane explanation for the foregrounded nature of these events in Mary's memoirs as opposed to the others'. Alice Clark and Edith Cold did go down initially to see what was happening and discovered that the "officials" of Hadjin did not know it had happened at all. But it was Mary and Edith Cold who went down later, to the building where the Turks were being held, accompanied by Turkish women, wives and daughters of the imprisoned men. Mary says that the Turkish mayor had been protecting the Turkish prisoners, and when he was replaced, conditions deteriorated. In an uncharacteristically emotional entry, Mary confesses that she and Edith witnessed "terrible sights": "It was utterly impossible for us to sleep that night because, when we closed our eyes, things would come before us until it was simply awful. It is beyond my power to describe that night."

But Mary works very hard to explain what has happened. She and the other relief workers had been strongly directed to remain neutral in all events, and all of them mention repeatedly that this strategy probably saved their lives. Certainly, their neutrality was instrumental in the Turkish Nationalists' asking them to mediate between themselves and the Armenians in Hadjin.

35. Eby, *At the Mercy,* 101.
36. Clark, *Letters,* 113.

Mary's explanation for the Armenians' "turning the tables" is ambivalent, indeed conflicted. First she insists that it was not done by Christian Armenians in the city.[37] Then she considers all that the Armenians were made to suffer at the hands of the Turks: "They were having revenge for the terrible oppression they had been made to suffer at the hands of the Turks. We know too well how they were oppressed . . ." She repeats several times that the Armenians treated the Turks very cruelly, but in the same manner in which they were treated during the war. And her acknowledgment of this reality is not pro forma. She had gone to comfort the frightened orphans in the compound many nights during the fighting. She knew that the sounds of war were "horrible for those poor children after the exile many of them had experienced." But in the end, two protests enter her account. First, her pragmatism tells her that there would be Turkish reprisals for this act, and thus she objects: ". . . in return, the innocent Armenians must suffer and perhaps our little folks and teachers."

Even more interesting, in a truly disruptive moment in terms of discursive assumptions, Mary takes exception to a Christian claim made by the Armenians who later visit the compound to explain the imprisonment to the relief workers. When they say that they have done nothing in comparison with what they suffered in the past, and that God would see it that way, Mary retorts: "It was true that they had suffered beyond all human reason. But whether God would look at it in that light was not for them to say." Here, a universal Christianity does not transcend culturally imbued ethics of affront and retribution. And the claim to God's sanction of a particular set of ethics is contested. Mary dismisses the Armenian frame of reference, appealing to the inscrutibility of God's judgment, a commonplace of Christian moralism. But it is also apparent that a culturally unfamiliar definition of the Christian God is threatening to her. In other instances, Mary deals with her sense of alienation from those she is serving by infantilizing them, in comments like "another story which shows of their ignorance . . .", or in stories about the Armenians' unscientific and, in Mary's view, arbitrary approach to medicine, or in her recounting of similar jokes made by

---

37. The Armenian "city people" who come to explain the imprisonment to the relief workers later do refer to God, however, which certainly appears to imply that they were Christian. Perhaps the ones explaining were not the initial perpetrators.

Edith Cold: "Make the tablet a color to suit the Turkish eye."

These disjunctures align with the more traditional religious rhetoric and missionary ideology apparent in Mary's text. While the memoirs are filled with far fewer pious religious clichés than Blanche's, Mary doubtless shared the basic beliefs Blanche articulated. So, Mary explains that "prayer to the throne of God was what guided me in administering the medicine." She clearly envisioned a "mutual" Christian ethos, but one that was imposed West to East, and not vice versa: "Miss Cold took these little children, many of whom had never had a day's schooling in their lives, and with the help of fourteen Consecrated Christian Armenian teachers began to train these young lives, so that they might be able to take their places as Christian men and women."

On the other hand, Mary's accounts of Armenians also contain a good deal of reported speech. But it is still difficult to determine how much can be learned about Armenian attitudes towards the relief workers. The orphans and people of Hadjin voice a desire for American protection. For instance, four orphan boys appearing at the compound say, "Oh, we will sleep under the stars. We don't mind. We have done it for four years, only let it be American property." Mary also recounts a pronounced deferential posture. The Armenians are described as being sorry that the Americans have to do so much work. When the Americans thank the Armenian teachers and girls for their services at the compound, they respond, "O, that is nothing to compare with what you are enduring for us." Patients, not wanting to dirty Mary's bandages, take them off, at the expense of their own healing. A young Armenian girl refuses to let Mary wash bandages: "O, don't Miss Super, they are too dirty for you to touch."

On the other hand, there are some instances where American Christian intervention is problematic. A little Armenian girl, Rebecca, who had lived in a Turkish home during the exile, is a case in point. She speaks Turkish, some Armenian, and English. When she first comes to the compound, she describes her Turkish mother as "dry bones and blue eyes." Her biological Armenian mother, who had been taken into a different Turkish home during the exile, was reunited with Rebecca in that Turkish home. Then they were both sent back to Hadjin and separated again; her mother, to work in an Armenian home, Rebecca, to stay in the compound orphanage. Rebecca cries and wishes to go to her mother: "Take me back. My blood is boiling towards you but I want my mother." This is articulated in Turkish, using a Turkish expression that, according to Mary, indicates "much love," by an Armenian orphan yearning for her Armenian mother, and refusing American aid. But after a few weeks, Mary reports, "*our* little girl became very happy . . . you could not have paid her to leave our school." (italics mine)

A similar containment of Armenian difference, this time within the discourse of Christian forgiveness, occurs in the last pages of the memoirs. Young Armenian girls in the orphanage tell Mary, "It is hard to pray for people who have massacred your father in front of your eyes." Mary insists that Christ will help them "fill their lives" so that they will be able to do so, "and they did. Every one of those girls helped serve the Turks" by washing bandages, making pastry, doing laundry, and baking bread. Is this an instance of a universally embraced ideal of Christian forgiveness or historical and cultural differences among Christians silenced and contained?

Finally, what of the Turks? Turkishness and being Muslim are diversely defined and exist along a continuum in the memoirs, articulated by the trilingual voices of Armenian orphans who had lived in Turkish homes (already considered in the story of Rebecca), the voices of the Turkish villagers in Hadjin, and the voices and actions of the Turkish Nationalist soldiers. Furthermore, the Nationalists are not reductively portrayed; their diversity is clearly defined within the details of strategic negotiations as the siege goes on. The relief workers' ability to survive the two-month siege depended on their careful attention to and interpretation of the Nationalists' motives, practices, and internal dynamics. This vigilance has produced a text that analyzes the Nationalists' every move with great energy, albeit refracted through the fear and trauma of being held hostage by force.

In general, Mary's descriptions of the local Turks and Kurds are sympathetic and appreciative. Yet, they are very different from the depiction of "friendly" or "converted" Turks interspersed throughout the memoirs of Blanche and Alice. Several of Blanche's accounts are essentially novelistic, for example, her story of the "Snarly Kurd" who becomes their friend, or her description of the particularly frightening soldier whom she refers to as "the Black Circassian." When this Circassian soldier witnesses the relief workers crying over a very young

Kurdish boy, killed by some unruly soldiers, she has him exclaim, "Why, they *loved* him!" then allows her imagination free rein:

> The Black Circassian continued to gaze with puzzled eyes upon the scene. This was something altogether beyond him. He wondered if, after all, they were doing right in waging this war against the infidels, and for the first time a doubt crept into his mind. In the days that followed there was a marked change in this wicked man. . . . They no longer feared him. Instead of calling him "that awful Black Circassian," they called him "the Lamb."[38]

But Mary's stories are less elaborate and certainly less inventive. She may mention the emotions of others, but always in the form of reported speech. For instance, she describes those Turks who have been imprisoned as alternately sad, confused, and enraged, then tells of her encounter with one Turk whom she calls, "a friend of the compound." He had been "very kind to Miss Vaughan [former missionary] and Miss Cold" and now, in prison, was "so sad. He did not understand his fate and he said he had never been in sympathy with the cruelty practiced on the Armenians. He had even given part of his house to refugee Armenians." Later, when Mary and her companions are traveling across the mountains to Talas, Mary recounts that Kurdish villagers entertained, hosted, and fed them during their escape. In one scene, we see a devout Muslim community—"a large company were going through their devotions." When the travelers are left to sit for two hours while the Kurds pray, their Turkish guide becomes angry, slaps the villagers, threatens them, and then burns down one of their homes. Mary and the others cannot eat because of this violent encounter. Here, Mary's ignorance of what was really going on between the Turks and Kurds in this village is a hindrance, since in general these two groups are represented as allies in the Nationalist campaign.

As for the Nationalist soldiers with whom the relief workers negotiated for two months, the exchanges, as narrated, generate a litany of conventional racist assertions and mistrust, but also some instances of

---

38. Eby, *At the Mercy*, 158-59.

rapprochement, alignment of interests, even mutual respect. Mary explains, "The Nationalist forces were composed of seven leaders of robber bands, each man was supposed to have at his command one hundred men." As a group, these men remain under the general rubric "creatures," which she assigns to them when they first enter the parlor to search the compound: "Miss Cold escorted these creatures into our sitting room, for one could hardly call them men. I cannot describe their looks. I hope never to see fiercer looking ones again."

Mary knew that these men were probably also the perpetrators of the Marash massacre, that "awful reign of terror." She also describes them in terms of proverbial sayings, whose authority is twofold, enhanced as they are by their traditional nature and carrying much popular weight among the Turks themselves and Armenians. So, her understanding of the Turks is amplified and authorized by hearsay: "The Turks say the guns are too good for the Christian dogs." "There is a saying that where there is not a desert where a Turk goes, he will soon make one." That these sayings emerge out of a long history of ethnic competition and hostility is obvious. To see Mary reproduce them is to see a kind of essentializing orientalism at work.

These men, the "angry," "dirty," "fierce" robber band leaders, are distinguished in the memoirs from the top commanders of the Nationalist forces, Enver and Jevan Bey, and also from the rank and file soldiers, "villagers" whom Mary suggests are anxious to get back home: "It was getting very warm and the villagers' crops and herds were being neglected." The latter group is also depicted as devout, especially during Ramadan in May: "They were celebrating their fast. . . . There was much made of the feast of Ramadan and the poor villagers were getting very restless to get home to their villages to attend this feast."[39] In line with this reading, the leaders control their men by citing religious principles: "As you love God and the prophet Mohammed, stay where you are."

In the Nationalists' concern for the Turks whom they know have been imprisoned in the town, particular, positioned values—cultural, ethnic, and religious—surface in their repeated requests that the Amer-

---

39. Mary is not mistaken about this timing. The dates of Ramadan move back approximately 10 days each year. May–June 1920 corresponds precisely with the month of Ramadan in the corresponding Islamic year, 1338.

icans serve as mediators between themselves and the Armenians, and in the specific conventions of alliance that they bring to their exchanges with the relief workers. They do not attack the compound. In return they expect honest disclosure of what is happening and neutrality in the Westerners' dealings with the Armenians and themselves. Enver Bey helps Miss Cold dig a garden bed and plants seeds with her in return for the medical care he receives from Mary, who saved his life. The Turks also tell (reassure?) the Americans that their countrymen are trying to reach them: "We knew the Americans were trying to reach us, for the Turks told us so." Finally, the Turkish commander refuses to have dinner at the compound, but this is, apparently, an act of integrity. Mary explains: "It is against Turkish etiquette to break bread with anyone whom in the future they might harm," but he says that if all went well after the siege, he would do so. And it is Enver who in the end saves them, by spiriting them out of the compound and up over the mountains, back to safety, when the compound is burned to the ground. Indeed, all along Mary describes Enver as protecting them from "the wild hordes of men surrounding us."

So Mary creates a portrait of a diverse coalition of Turks and Kurds, villagers and commanders, devout and destructive men. She never reproduces Turkish speech at the level of hostility reported in Blanche's story, when the Nationalists feel betrayed: "'These curs of Christians,' cried the angry mob! 'Why are they kept here under our nose? Their very presence is polluting. They bring bad luck, disaster, and destruction upon us. Let every one of the accursed race die, and may Allah consign them to eternal torment!'"[40] Nor does Mary recount the kind of cross-cultural flexibility and play that Blanche does. In one instance, Blanche describes a gathering of the Turkish *beys* (leaders) around her husband, when they are asking him to mediate on their behalf with the

---

40. Eby, *At the Mercy*, 194. An even more pronounced and politically revealing example, this time of Kurdish hostility, occurs in the final pages of Blanche's narrative. As the relief workers make their way across the mountains to safety, they are hosted by a variety of Turkish and Kurdish dignitaries, including a "Sheyk" and an "ex-Governor" in a Kurdish village, who get drunk and indulge in anti-imperialist strategizing in their presence, "utterly unconscious of the missionaries": "'We do not want foreigners in our country,' said the ex-Governor. 'True, we need them to teach us how to develop our resources, and we must invite some of them to be our instructors. We shall have to endure their presence for four or five years, but after that they must go.' . . . 'We will drive out every one of them: drive them out without mercy,' agreed the Sheyk" (270).

Armenians once again. They conclude, "Meudir Effendi is not an Armenian; neither is he an American any longer. He has become a *chete* (brigand), and he is now one of ourselves."[41] This claiming of alliance is manipulative and strategic, and the missionaries know it. Reverend Eby returns to the ladies in the compound with his *chete* hat on, saying, "I am a brigand chief!" The irony and duplicity are amplified by the fact that, to ensure his safety, the Westerners had hidden Eby's Canadian citizenship from the Turks, claiming he was an American.

Another example of strategic alliance, this one from Alice's letters, involves an angry search of the compound by the Turks, who felt the Americans had deceived them and hidden soldiers on the premises. When the search is ended and they leave, Edith Cold does not want them to leave angry:

> She turned to him [the man who had been most angry] and said, "Achmet, you have a future in the world and I have a future and we must live together in this world. How can we go on if there is hatred in our hearts." She put out her hand and laid it on his shoulder. It wasn't pleasant for he was dirty but, holding her hand there and looking straight into his eyes, she said solemnly, "By this touch, I make you my brother. Now, if you are my brother and I am your sister, we must do good to one another and not evil." Achmet looked at her and, as if her touch had magic in it, his face softened and, gazing at her, he replied, "It is in truth so."[42]

This exchange embraces aphoristic wisdom and religious concepts in the interest of a strategic political alliance, alongside class disdain and a mystification of patronage (almost a branding of the Turk as belonging to the American). This branding is figured as "magic," with the added implication that Christian brotherhood is implanted in the Muslim brother through the magic grace of God.

---

41. Eby, *At the Mercy*, 182.
42. Clarke, *Letters*, pp. 145-46.

Concluding Remarks

It is in fits and starts that the people in Mary's memoirs reach toward "common ethical and ideational bases for connection,"[43] if not a universal shared identity. The memoirs reveal competing loyalties embedded in conflicting identities and accidental, sometimes forced affiliations that evoke complicity and resistance, cruelty and altruism. The impulse towards connection is there in the disciplined neutrality of the Near East Relief workers, the regret and resignation of Turks who had helped Armenians and continued to sympathize with them, the chivalry of the wounded Enver Bey planting seeds for Edith Cold, a woman alone, without men on the compound to do the heavy lifting. And it is challenged in the cultural rifts that erupt intermittently and unexpectedly throughout the memoirs in the guise of racism, distrust, projection, confusion, idealization, cooptation, violence—rifts that defy universalist assumptions and thwart interreligious understanding. The old ideal of Ottoman universalism or cosmopolitanism may have been giving way to Turkish and Armenian nationalism. Nevertheless, the interpersonal and strategic use of religious, national, and gendered identities to create "common cause" in the memoirs demonstrates the persistence of both ideals in 1920 Hadjin. Ironically, both the Christian and Islamic religions make a claim in the memoirs to universal relevance and applicability.

And so, Mary's concluding paragraphs are different in tone from the rest of her text, as she moves to a macro analysis of her experience: "If you think of a Nation who has worshipped a man, or Mohammed the Prophet, for centuries, you have a picture of the Turks." These final paragraphs are particularly revealing as an unintentional summary of her *own* cultural and religious assumptions. Reading them, one can clearly see that she steadfastly believed that Islam was misguided, and that the Turkish and Kurdish Muslims she met were lost, not saved. She clearly hoped that all Muslims would learn about Jesus and convert to Christianity, and she ends her memoirs with a confession of her own pity for the Turks. Of the array of roles that Mary took on so far from

---

43. Mohammed Bamyeh, "Global Order and the Historical Structures of Dar al-Islam," in *Rethinking Globalism,* ed. Manfred Steger (Lanham, MD: Rowman and Littlefield, 2004), 221-22.

home—scientist, independent woman, doctor, friend, mother to orphans, Christian—it is the Christian who has the last word, moralistic, compassionate, missionizing, self-sacrificing, and hopeful. It is, thus, misleading to overemphasize the presence of conflicting discourses in her memoirs. Neither Mary, nor Blanche, nor Alice shows any sign of having rethought her beliefs or purpose in any substantial way over the course of her experiences. Neither do any of the Turks or Kurds or Armenians in Mary's memoirs. When epiphanies and conversions to Christian sentimentality in a Turk or Kurd occur in Blanche's memoirs, they clearly belong to the sentimental genre of Christian mission, "converting the heathen," and their accuracy is dubious. In the end, the memoirs testify to the persistence and resilience of cultural and religious beliefs and identities, even as they demonstrate their elasticity in extremis, within particularly conflictual historical circumstances.

The Memoirs

Entered the service for the Near East Relief as a Red Cross Nurse on January 29, 1919 and sailed from Hoboken on the *Leviathan* on the 16th of February. This vessel, which was formerly known as the "Fatherland" (Germany's largest vessel), was then employed by our navy as a transport.[44]

We arrived in Brest on February 23rd. At Brest there was nothing to be seen but mud, and plenty of rain, and homesick American boys.

Leaving Brest on the evening of February 23rd, we crossed France to Marseilles in a Red Cross Hospital train, taking the regular soldier fare.

We arrived in Marseilles at noon on February 26th where we were told that we were to go to the "Gloucester Castle," an English Hospital ship which had been waiting for our party for one day and a half.

March 5th and 6th we were in Salonica or old Thessalonica. The British entertained us one day sightseeing. The indescribable poverty of that city as a result of the war was pitiful.

---

44. Joseph Grabill, *Protestant Diplomacy and the Near East: Missionary Influence on American Policy, 1810-1927* (Minneapolis: University of Minnesota Press, 1971), 165-66, reports that in February 1919, the U.S. Navy shipped 2,000 tons of flour, 2,500 cases of canned foods, 500 cases of condensed milk, 18 trucks, 20 ambulances, 500 sewing machines, 200 oil stoves, 1,750,000 yards of cloth, 50,000 blankets, 800 hospital cots, 26 tents, 78 X-ray machines, and 200 tons of coal. (This list is reproduced in Donald E. Miller and Lorna Touryan Miller, *Survivors: An Oral History of the Armenian Genocide* [Berkeley and Los Angeles: University of California Press, 1993], 121.) Miller and Miller also verify that the *Leviathon* left New York on February 16, carrying "240 mission and relief personnel, including 30 physicians and 60 nurses," of the last of which Mary was obviously one.

Our party, numbering 240[45], arriving in Constantinople unexpectedly caused some commotion. It was decided to send all nurses and as many relief workers as possible out to Prinkipo, a lovely island down the Bosporus where the committee opened up the hotels for our entertainment.

On March 16th, I left Prinkipo on a U.S. sub-chaser for Derindje, an island in the Marmora, where we lived on the fifth floor of a warehouse, fitted up as a dormitory. Our work here was to help check up stock and superintend the loading of cars, especially getting the canned milk out to the starving, while we were waiting for our assignments.

On April 17th, I left for Adana, a mission station in Cilicia, Asia Minor, where I was a nurse in an industrial home for refugee girls. These girls went through almost indescribable tortures during the years of exile. Miss Webb, the missionary,[46] really showed them what a true home was, Near East Relief supporting this home. If the Americans could only have visited the home, they would have known how worthwhile was the drive for funds in America.

On June 17th, I left Adana for Hadjin, a mountain town in Cilicia, Asia Minor. From Adana, it was a ride of a day and a half by native carriage. The day began at two-thirty in the morning. We reached Sis at eight in the morning. After resting for a few hours, our party went out sightseeing around that interesting old city. It was one of the battlefields of Alexander the Great. We expected to leave on Tuesday evening but were unable to secure animals until Thursday evening. From Sis to Hadjin the only means of transportation was "*araba*" (Turkish name for ox-cart), camel, or horseback. It was three days' journey.

My work in Hadjin was to hold a public clinic and make any out calls for those too sick to get to me. Our clinic was the only adequate

---

45. Mary confirms that 240 volunteers shipped together out of Hoboken. This group is also referred to as "the *Leviathan* party" by the Near East Relief in its tribute to 1,000 volunteers who served overseas: Charles Vickrey, *Teamwork: A Tribute and an Appeal*, ed. Mabell S. C. Smith (New York: Near East Relief National Headquarters Publication, 1924). See Appendix F.2.

46. An Elizabeth S. Webb and a Mary G. Webb are both listed in Vickrey, *Teamwork*, as volunteers returned from overseas by 1924 for whom the Near East Relief had no address. These two were both listed as having been in Beirut, however. It's possible that one of them is Mary's "Miss Webb," and that she transferred to Beirut later.

medical help for about five months for about 15 villages. This clinic was under the direction of the American doctor at Adana. Four days from a doctor is a long way when you need immediate help and advice, but prayer to the throne of God was what guided me in administering the medicine when at sea to know just what would help most, for we Americans must not fail those in need. The people in the East feel if they can only get American medicine, that is all that is necessary.

Our supplies gave out during the winter and Adana was not always able to meet our needs. I had a woman sit in the road for two hours insisting on having our medicine. She had a very heavy cold. I advised her to go to the Armenian Hospital, but she said, "Just give me any American medicine." When she would not go and it was growing dark I did give her a remedy which I did not think would help her need, but she went away happy and in a week returned to thank me for our good medicine, saying it had helped the whole family.

Turkish women were always coming to call on Miss Cold, the missionary.[47] They came in groups of five or six. Then they would ask for me. They would tell Miss Cold of their numerous complaints, and if they were not paying for the medicine I would scarcely know which medicine would be the best to select for the present need.

Miss Cold was a missionary and also director of the station for Near East Relief. We decided that those who could pay for the medicine should pay a small sum, and by doing this we found that we obtained a more definite idea of just what ailed them. The most interesting part of the visit would be when we would give out the medicine. They would compare the remedies. Great care must be taken not to give the same remedy to any two women of the same party. If I felt that the remedy was not just what one would prescribe, under other circumstances, I would invite the patient back, making the visit very important. Of course, it would please the patient that you were so interested in them. Miss Cold often said, "If the people in America only knew, she was sure they would have been very glad to make the tablet a color to suit the Turkish eye." The Near East Relief never turned anyone away, feeling that in this way we could protect the Armenians by being on friendly terms with the Turks.

---

47. Edith Cold, of Oberlin, Ohio. See Appendix F.2 for Edith's entry in *Teamwork*.

Another very interesting thing which they would do was to bring a sample of the medicine or ointment which had helped them. One woman had been helped by a pink pill which Miss Vaughan, a former missionary,[48] had given her six years before. The pink color suited her eye as well as the disease. After keeping the tablet for six years, her little girl had a similar complaint and she returned with the sample for her remedy. As Miss Cold knew the customs of the natives better than I did, I asked her advice. She said no matter what you would substitute for that pill, nothing in her mind would be of any value. So Mary, my helper, a young Armenian schoolgirl, who Miss Vaughan had trained as her assistant, knew where a small supply of the favorite remedy was kept. This was brought, and our patient went away pronouncing many blessings on us. Miss Clark, one of our associates,[49] said, "She had heard of samples for many things but never for medicine," and I am sure no one else has.

Life is so cheap in the East. A wife or baby can soon be replaced, and old age is not respected. One day a mother came crying into my clinic with her two-year-old child in her arms. I tried to find out what the trouble was. She said, "Oh, Doctor, if my baby is going to die, please tell me and I will not trouble you anymore." The baby's tongue had a streak of black on it, and its little feet were swollen. Some old native woman had told her that it would surely die. I told her how sorry I was for her and asked her what her baby had eaten. She said she did not know. The mother has nothing to say about her children or her home; she is entirely under the direction of her mother-in-law who is head of the home (oriental custom). Although they nurse their babies they also give them an adult's diet from the time they are very young. I cleansed the baby's tongue and found that the streak washed off. Then I gave her a remedy and told her to bring the baby just as often as she wished or I would come to see it, that in America we never stop caring for the babies until the case is entirely hopeless or cured, while they just stop feeding them.

---

48. Mary says that Miss Vaughn was a missionary who had been at "the school," presumably in Hadjin, during the war. She is not listed in any sources I have used.

49. Alice Keep Clark, of Evanston, Illinois. See Appendix F.2 for Alice's entry in *Teamwork*. See also her published memoirs, *Letters from Cilicia* (Chicago: A. D. Weinthrop & Co., 1924).

One afternoon a woman came into my clinic asking for medicine for her mother. She was given all the necessary instructions and we had told her to let us hear from her the next day. We heard nothing from her for weeks until one day she came back to return something which she had borrowed. I inquired how her mother was, and she said, "She is dead. Your medicine helped her and she got up and worked for a few days. Then she was taken sick again, so we thought, 'why trouble the doctor?', if she was not going to be well all the time." The mother had lain ten days without medicine and perhaps with very little food. The medicine which I had given her was just enough for two days as they do everything according to the sun, and the medicine had to be arranged so they could take it three times daily. If it is necessary to give more, an out call is made.

We had fifteen outlying villages under our care, Hadjin being the central front.

Another story which shows of their ignorance: If they have means and need medical attention, they would call in all the doctors in town and one doctor is kept in perfect ignorance of the other's visit. They take the medicine which tastes the best or, as they would express it, that which their "soul desires."

When they hold a consultation in the East, if the family is wealthy and they can secure a dozen doctors, all present make a diagnosis of the case. They sit around in a circle all writing out a prescription.

This story was told me by the mission doctor at Adana when he knew I would have to take a doctor's place in Hadjin, advising me never to go where medicine had already been administered and to be very careful of these conventions.

People coming from the villages sometimes on foot or on the donkey were not always able to make the trip in one day.

I had two helpers—one an Armenian teacher, who was my interpreter, and Mary, a young Armenian schoolgirl, who was surely my right hand.

During July and August, I treated at the clinic 4,220 patients for scabies or itch, which was very prevalent after the war; syphilis; eye troubles; and numerous other such diseases. It is a very common thing to see people in the East blind or suffering with serious eye diseases. T.B., most dreaded by them, abounds. Their custom is to abandon them, through fear of contagion.

While our clinic was a busy place, our relief work played a large part in our busy life at Hadjin, for when Miss Cold and Miss MacLean, a Red Cross Nurse who opened the clinic in Hadjin[50], arrived early in April, the refugees were a pitiful sight. Their clothing just hung on them in rags.

Through the funds given to the Near East Relief by the American people, it was possible for Miss Cold and Miss Vaughan, the missionary who had been at the school during the war, to give clothing to these poor refugees. But clothing was not given promiscuously where work could be given the people. In exchange for the work, they were either given money or material, whichever they preferred, to keep up the Armenian spirit of independence.

Early in May, Miss Clark arrived. Then, she and Miss Cold carried on the relief work with the help of the native teachers.

With the returning of the refugees, the relief work had grown to gigantic proportions. At five or six o'clock in the morning we would have great crowds at the gate. At times our gatekeeper would be overpowered and it would be necessary for Miss Clark to control the mob.

On certain days, the wool was given out. This was carded, spun, or knitted into stockings for our children.[51] Then two days of the week, the orphans were received. This became a crying need. Although we had inadequate quarters, children were coming back as refugees without a relative or friend—but the Near East Relief. Only such children were received as applicants. Those who had mothers were given work and a small sum of money to provide for their food. We had four or five hundred children supported in this way. With this, and the income from the labor, these families were able to live. Work was provided by the Near East Relief Committee, weaving native goods (rugs) and building shelter for our children.

When four little boys applied at the school for admittance, and we told them that we did not have sufficient quarters at that time to share

---

50. This may be C. M. MacLean, Nurse, of Ontario, Canada, who was listed in Vickrey, *Teamwork*, as still serving overseas in Oropos in 1924.

51. Miller and Miller, *Survivors: An Oral History*, 129-30, indicate that, "orphans also did needlework for their sponsors in the United States." They quote an orphan survivor describing her day: "We used to study and go to school until noon. In the afternoon, we had to do needlework. They used to tell us that the work we did they sent to the United States, so the Americans would send money with which we could be fed."

with them, they said, "Oh, we will sleep out under the stars. We don't mind. We have done it for four years, only let it be American property." This they did for four days until a place was found for them.

A factory was started where the native goods were woven. Of course this supplied many with work. There was a store where both American and native goods were sold. Then our orphanage was open. The boys were sent up to Mr. Eby's[52] vineyard, and the little girls had the upper part of the factory. They lived in these quarters until the middle of September when the girls occupied the clinic building until December. Then a nice dormitory was finished which made our clinic building a three-story building. The older girls slept here, while the younger ones slept in the lower rooms with the housemother. Seventeen girls were housed in the main building of our school. These were Armenian children.

When school opened on the first of October our boys were brought to the factory building, which was occupied during the summer by the few little girls which we had.

As Mr. and Mrs. Eby and Miss Brademons, the Mennonite missionaries, had returned[53], Mr. Eby and a native helper took over the factory which was now self-supporting. There was a great transformation in the appearance of the people—instead of rags, they were clothed and earning a living.

During the early fall Miss Cold and Miss Clark toured the village, supplying their needs for the winter and bringing the little ones to the orphanage. What a sorry lot they were. These poor children, with most of the older people, had been in exile for four years, starved, ill treated, and subjected to every kind of exposure. They were ragged, dirty and covered with all kinds of vermin—sometimes wearing only a burlap bag. Their cleansing bath upon admittance was the first one they had probably ever known. Many of them were covered with the itch.

---

52. D. C. Eby, Canadian Mennonite missionary and husband of Blanche Remington Eby. See the Introduction, above.

53. D. C. Eby, his wife, Blanche, and a Miss Bredemus are all mentioned in Rose Lambert's account of the 1909 massacres in Hadjin: *Hadjin and the Armenian Massacres* (New York: Fleming H. Revell Company, 1911). She identifies them as "our missionaries" in Hadjin at that time, along with several others who died. There is a picture of the group in her book, and in that photo the Ebys look quite a bit younger than they do in the photos in Blanche's memoirs. It would have been almost exactly a decade before. This may account for Mary's using the word "returned."

Miss Clark, then having finished the relief work, was the director of the orphanage, and what a big mother she made. I don't think any little girls in America had a happier time. She, personally, superintended the making of the clothing, saw that they were provided with some play things, although not many.

Miss Cold took these little children, many of whom had never had a day's schooling in their lives, and with the help of fourteen Consecrated Christian Armenian teachers began to train these young lives, so that they might be able to take their places as Christian men and women.

We lived among these children and were happy to see them grow. We went down every Wednesday night and took supper with them so they might feel that we were interested in them.

In the latter part of September the grapes were gathered, cleaned, and pressed. In the East they are pressed with their feet. The grapes are stemmed and placed in a large receptacle. In our school two of the teachers stamped the grapes. After they are all pressed out, the juice is put into a large boiler. It is boiled and made into "pechnez" or syrup, which resembles our molasses. It is boiled four hours. English Walnuts are opened and the halves strung on a string and dipped into this boiling syrup. They are placed on a nail to dry and used as a native candy. While they are boiling the syrup, the children sing songs and play games until midnight.

Little Rebecca was a little girl who had only been in our school for a short time. When her mother was exiled, the child was only three years old. She was separated from her parents, her father being sent away as a soldier and her mother exiled. She was then placed in a Turkish home to rock the baby's cradle. When asked if she liked her mistress, she said, "No. She was dry bones and blue eyes." Stout people are more popular in the East. After the war was over, the mother was a servant in a high Turkish official's home. She wept often about her baby until her master asked her why she was weeping. Then she told him about her baby. He sent word to the official of the village where the baby was, to one who held the same office as he. They found little Rebecca still there. This friend was advised to send her by the postman. You can imagine the joyful reunion of little Rebecca and her mother. However they were not together long for all Armenians who wished to leave their Turkish homes were given free transportation by the British and little Rebecca came to Hadjin and her mother was a servant for an Armenian family.

At first she was very unhappy at our school. She would cry and say, "Take me back; take me back just for tonight." Our little folks tried to comfort her by telling her how much they loved her. She would say, "My blood is boiling towards you but I want my mother." It was a Turkish expression meaning much love. After the weeks of homesickness had worn off, our little girl became very happy. By November you could not have paid her to leave our school.

In November we had such a nice birthday party. Our honored guest, Miss Waryham,[54] was at this time in America on a furlough. She was the missionary who had stayed with these people and was much loved by them. We had about two hundred and twenty five guests present. Our dining room was decorated with autumn leaves and young pines. We had lamb, roasted whole, in the native way, and all the native dishes which accompany this kind of a feast, as we would say "a fatted calf feast." Lamb is only served this way when one wishes to show great honor and respect to the guest. We had a large birthday cake for the guests and cookies for the children. An appropriate program was given in the evening. One of the happy features of the day for the children was when we gathered the decorations. They knew nothing of the coming of the Turks. They sang and laughed as they pulled up the small pines. How they uprooted them I could not say. They gathered the autumn leaves and climbed over those mountains without the least difficulty.

Little Rebecca who had been so unhappy before was now having a wonderful time. I heard someone singing in Turkish, "I Know He Died for Me" and turned around and there was the dear little girl. These little folks made such a lovely picture coming into the compound yard that Miss Clark took their photograph. The children certainly had a delightful time. This party had made the children so happy that we decided to have another one in February for someone whom they should remember in the same way.

---

54. This woman is not listed in any sources I have consulted.

We had a nice Christmas party for them. The little boys asked for pens, and the little girls for bags. Although we could not grant the request of the boys at present, we could later in the winter. But Miss Cold called them together and told them the circumstances. Miss Clark and Miss Cold made it possible for them to have a small bag of Christmas goodies. The Christmas tree was trimmed, but we in America would not look at those trimmings. Nevertheless, when Miss Cold had them arranged, they were really very pretty.

We had expected a nice Christmas box from Chicago but the vessel went down at sea. In return, they gave us a nice Christmas play, and on Christmas morning at five o'clock I heard a commotion at my room door. Very shortly after this they began singing the Christmas carols. After they had finished, fifteen young girls came around to the alcove, where my bed was standing, to wish me "A Merry Christmas" and what a sight it was, each holding a lighted candle. Don't you think you would have enjoyed such a Christmas morning? They went around to visit Miss Cold and Miss Clark, and as my room was next to the dormitory I received the first visit.

We had two Merry Christmas placards in each of our rooms. The words on the placards, which were made by the little girls, were not always written straight or spelled correctly. These were shaded with a colored pencil and were placed in our rooms early in the morning.

The little orphan boys did their part, making a placard and pasting it on the front gate of the compound. What a funny one it was! I wish you could have seen it.

We were all happy leading this sort of a life and it was a very busy one indeed. Miss Cold would often laugh and say we did not grow tired of each other's company because we seldom saw each other except at the table.

But by the middle of January [1920], the rumors of the coming of the Turks, as soon as the snow was melted so they could get through the mountain passes, brought a sudden gloom over our happy family, because they knew from past experience just what the coming of the Turks meant. It was with great difficulty that Miss Cold conducted her school, spending a great deal of time in the sitting room. She still persevered in carrying on the school because we hoped that in some way these rumors were false. Miss Cold kept many of these rumors away from our children for many of them had seen and heard too much in the years of exile. Many of our girls and boys, although they were ten or twelve years of age, had never had a day of schooling. Consequently, Miss Cold was determined that the school should be open as long as it possibly could.

[In] our graduating class were girls eligible to enter the college at Constantinople. Only one of the girls received the scholarship to the college, but others were sent elsewhere to finish their education. The people in America can never realize what a fearful nervous strain was upon Miss Cold, caused by the school work and the coming of the Nationalists; also the numerous conferences which she must hold with the Armenians for they thought that she must hear every rumor. She alone could dictate the telegrams which they demanded to be sent to the French in Sis and finally to Adana, that we were unduly alarmed.

The Turks sent several letters demanding the removal of the French flag from the Armenian school. This the Armenians refused to do, saying that they had not placed it there and they refused to take it down. It had been placed on the school by the Army of Occupation when they effectively occupied Hadjin on the 9th of July, 1919. The Turks promised the Armenians protection if they would only remove the flag and let the nationalists come through Hadjin unharmed. But the Armenians refused to do this because from past experience they had learned not to trust the Turks and one could not blame them for doing so. The French had armed them, sometimes with the arms and ammunition taken from the Turks, and you can imagine the effect on the Turks, thus giving the Armenians license to oppress the Turks. But, oh, they could not be blamed for they had gone through so much more than we American people would believe possible.

On January 21st, hostilities began with a massacre in Marash[55], a city of three days' journey by horseback from Hadjin.

On February 3rd, very alarming rumors were received at the compound. Miss Cold told us that evening, if they were all true, it would only be a providence of God if we were all alive by the middle of May.

After the Marash massacre things grew more tense. Marash was a large place which was inhabited by both Armenians and Turks. It was

---

55. Cf. Kerr, *Lions of Marash.*

just on the outskirts of Cilicia and during the war it was garrisoned by the English. But when the French took Cilicia, they also took over Marash, which the Turks or the Nationalists claimed. This caused the awful reign of terror from January 21st until February 12th or 15th. The Turks on the inside of the city massacred the Armenians and the Nationalists keeping guard so that those from within could not escape.

On February 11th we were making an official visit to the hospital because as things grew more tense it became necessary for us to do all we could for the people. We went out every day to cheer them. They, as we all know, had great confidence in the protecting power of the Americans.

Mr. Seeley of the Near East Relief from Adana[56] was up to find out the needs of the people of Hadjin and to distribute blankets among the poor. He also came to inquire into the needs of the outlying villages. On our return it was rumored that messengers had come from Marash. Before we reached our compound, Miss Cold was handed a letter telling of the awful reign of terror in that region. This letter was from the Armenian pastor telling of the massacre of his wife and two little sons along with many others.

When we reached our compound we found three men who had been sent out by Dr. Wilson, the director of the Near East Relief in Marash, asking for help. Six men had volunteered to carry this message to Miss Cold but only three had reached Hadjin. What pitiful creatures they were, ragged, worn, and discouraged for they had met with great difficulties on their way. It was necessary for them to secure what rest they could during the day because they must go from mountain peak to mountain peak during the night, the trip being made more hazardous because of the heavy fall of snow during the winter. These men volunteered to make this trip for twenty gold Turkish pounds or between eighty and ninety dollars in our money. This telegram stated the need for American money and food and asked that the American Consul be notified.[57]

_____

56. An Earl H. Seeley was listed in Vickrey, *Teamwork*, among the volunteers returned from overseas by 1924 for whom the Near East Relief had no address.

57. In Blanche's memoirs, only two men arrive at Hadjin, carrying the telegram bound for Aleppo. In Blanche's account, the telegram reads as follows: "To the American Consul, Aleppo: Situation in Marash extremely desperate. Reign of terror in city since Jan. 21st.

On February 12th, Mr. Seeley left Hadjin and invited us to come to Adana, saying that perhaps it was our last chance of getting away. Although we thought so too, we stayed with our children. The children thought that we surely could protect them. But some of our household wrote what they thought perhaps might be their last letters to their relatives and friends in America.

Mr. Seeley thought he might be able to do more for us in Adana than Hadjin, as Dr. Dodd[58] and he might be able to stir the French to action. But even the European nations move slowly in the East. Unfortunately, messages intended for Armenians were dropped from airplanes and fell into the hands of the Turks.

Our next communication from the French advised that all the women and children leave Hadjin. We were to walk to a village which was a six-hour journey on horseback from Hadjin. At this village, the French were to meet us with a force of two hundred soldiers.

Mr. Eby had at that time some fifty or sixty children at the Armenian orphanage and we had about two hundred and twenty. They, including our school children, ranged from five to twenty years of age.

We Americans had horses but there was no other means of transportation provided, unless we would have been able to strap the children to our backs and, even then, there would not have been enough backs for all.

After a conference we decided that we must stay with our little ones and wait till help came.

On February 19th, we had a birthday surprise party. This time our honored guest was present. We just had the school children and teachers and the orphan girls for supper. The boys came up with the teacher and housemother in the evening. An appropriate program was given. It was considered a success and our little folks all went to bed happy.

Hundreds of men, women, and children massacred daily. No power to stop this, as French are strictly on the defensive. Forces and munitions inadequate. Americans have little hope if French are overpowered, as soldiers defend from our compound. No assurance of help, as large forces bar all roads. Leave nothing undone to relieve situation, as lives of all Christians are seriously threatened. Our auto and flag fired upon repeatedly. Our institutions under fire, and many refugees and orphans wounded. Food short. Notify Arnold and Bristol. Wilson" (Eby, *At the Mercy*, 95).

58. Dr. William S. Dodd of Montclair, NY, who was listed in Vickrey, *Teamwork*, as still serving overseas as "Director" in Konia in 1924.

We planned this party hoping to take the awful gloom and terror of the coming of the Turks from our children's minds for a short time at least.

On February 22nd, a commission of Armenians left Hadjin for Adana, after being warned by a friendly Turk of the approach of the Nationalists. They had a thrilling experience. Two of their horses were shot from under them but the riders fortunately escaped. After concealing themselves in a hole for several hours they reached Sis safely. The French were not even stirred by this thrilling experience. They left for Adana, a strong French center, and after much discussion they promised to send an aeroplane up to Hadjin every forty-eight hours. The first one came over our compound the first week in March.

On February 26th, we, according to the custom of the Armenians, celebrated the burning of winter all over the town. If one would pass through the town on the 26th of February, you would see preparations being made for a large bonfire. Just as soon as it grows dark the fires are lighted with great ceremony. Then the children sing and play ring-games around the fire. Just as the fire is dying they jump back and forth over it. Miss Clark and I had never seen this ceremony before. She said that she feared that she would have to mend their clothing and I their bodies. But Miss Cold assured us that they were safe, and it was so nice to watch the children really enjoy life for a short time. Next day the women started to prepare little plots of ground for seed.

On March 5th, there was an attack on Romlow, a village only a short distance from Hadjin—about four hours horseback ride.

After the Armenians were armed they oppressed the Turks.[59] One never oppresses the Turks but that they seek revenge in a threefold way. The villages called on the Nationalists for help. Hostility had really started—all the Armenians fled to Hadjin and were housed with friends or in Armenian schools.

On March 8th, all Turks were imprisoned in the American building, which was then used as a Y.M.C.A. This was not done by the Christian

---

59. It is not altogether clear what Mary is referring to here, or where these Turks were "oppressed." As noted in Appendix C.5, it is possible that she is referring to members of the ARF-*Dashnak* party, since the Armenian Revolutionary Federation (ARF) organized itself into small armed resistance groups (*fedayees*) and, among other things, attempted to defend Armenian towns and villages. In this case, Mary would be reporting in this paragraph that the villages were appealing to *Armenian* Nationalists for help.

Armenians of Hadjin.[60] All felt that the move was indeed a serious one. Miss Cold was notified of this and she and Miss Clark went down to the building. I could not accompany them because I had to make a call on a very sick woman and, as we had a little boy who was just passing through the crisis of pneumonia, it was necessary for someone to watch him very closely. I met Miss Cold and Miss Clark going down the hill from our compound and they said that they had left Mary, my helper, with our sick boy, saying that they were not sure when they might return.

When Miss Cold and Miss Clark arrived at the Y.M.C.A. the Turks were all glad to see them. There was not a male Turk in Hadjin— all male Turks entering Hadjin that morning were imprisoned. The villagers had come in with produce that morning. They also had great confidence in Miss Cold's ability to help them and were very glad to be in our building.

When they arrived at the Y.M.C.A. they noticed that none of the officials of Hadjin were present, and when Miss Cold sent for them she found that they knew nothing about the happenings of the morning. The Turks were all moved to the Government building and they felt very resentful about it. But we had been advised by Admiral Bristol in Constantinople (he then represented our American government) to stay absolutely neutral no matter what the circumstances might be.

The Armenians protected the Turks, as they had promised, for about two weeks. Then, the *Commacum*[61] was put out of office because he was trying to protect the Turks. As a revenge, the Turks, who were then ruling a village from six to eight hours ride on horseback from Hadjin, cut off communication to Hadjin.

On March 15th, the telegraph wires were cut and we were thus entirely cut off from the outside world.

On March 21st, Miss Cold took in our first refugees—a family of five. We had constant visits to our clinic asking for strength medicine and medicine for fright.

---

60. Here, Mary may be distinguishing the local Armenians who lived in Hadjin from Armenian soldiers (or *fedayees*) who had come from the nearby town of Sis, with the French, to protect Hadjin. It is clear that she is describing the imprisonment of Turkish inhabitants of Hadjin and surrounding villages.

61. Mary glosses this word as a term for "mayor."

The Armenians asked if we wanted a guard on our road, but Miss Cold refused, saying that we were under the protection of our flag.

In October[62], about sixty volunteer, armed Armenian soldiers had come to Hadjin to live with the people. They were in the town until about the middle of January. Then the Governor General of Sis, then representing the French government, recalled one half of them. But from the time they arrived until they were recalled, they oppressed the Turks. The tables were turned and for a short time they were having revenge for the terrible oppression they had been made to suffer at the hands of the Turks.

We knew too well how they [the Armenians] were oppressed—their daughters forced to marry the Turks or made to live with the Moselem as his wife and slave. Some of them or their families were even buried alive or made to live in dark places called prisons. If you could only see one of those places, you would understand just what I mean. They were tortured by being compelled to live there at night or declare that they would turn Moselem, or march and work all day if they refused. This is just a few of the things they were made to suffer.

Sanitation in the East was practically unheard of except at the places where the American or European people lived. Consequently these prisons were very unhealthy places and in them all sorts of disease germs might breed.

Another very sad thing was the fact that they had gone through so much that they had lost interest in God or spiritual things. If they would turn Moselem, then they would be protected. But when an Armenian is a real believer, he would go through almost any kind of torture. He would even be willing to die, which many of them did during exile, in the past, and were still willing to do.

Many Armenians who turned Moselem during the years of the war

---

62. Over the next five paragraphs, Mary appears to be supplying background information to explain the imprisonment of the Turks by the town of Hadjin in March. She then returns to narrating Miss Cold's attempt to mediate between the groups. It's interesting that she clearly states it was not "Christian Armenians" who tortured the Turks in Hadjin. It seems to have been the "volunteer soldiers," the same ones who threatened Miss Cold's life later for being "pro-Turkish." Because Blanche Eby includes no helpful details of this sequence of events in her memoirs, we have no corresponding account to consult. Blanche states simply that, "The Armenians then imprisoned all the Turks in the city... gathered up the Turks and Kurds... as a precautionary measure" (*At the Mercy*, 101).

turned to the Gregorian faith after the war, or the native faith—a high church, similar to the Catholic faith in this country.

The Armenians treated the Turks very cruelly, in a manner similar to that which they had experienced during the war. Finally one of the Armenians from the neighboring village of Shar, whose little girl had been educated in our school, asked Miss Cold to go freely among the Turkish women of Hadjin and tell them that the Christian Armenians were not in sympathy with the awful things that were happening in town.[63]

It was on the evening of the 25th of March that Miss Cold told us of the interview and announced at the supper table that she would visit the Turkish women the following afternoon. We offered to accompany her but she refused, saying that she thought perhaps she could talk to them better alone as she was the only one of the three who spoke their language.

On the morning of the 26th, more rumors were brought to the compound. Miss Cold considered the matter and felt it best to invite us to accompany her. I was standing on the porch of the clinic building when she called from the porch of the school and asked me if I would not go with her. After making the necessary arrangements for the clinic during my absence, Miss Cold and I started out. We did not tell Miss Clark of our going for she had had some very trying work during the morning and was then resting.

As we were about to enter the first Turkish home, we were met at the entrance by the woman whom we hoped to visit first. She was accompanied by one of her friends. They invited Miss Cold and I to accompany them. We went down to the Government building and, as we walked, the Turkish women of the town, joined our party.

Our first friend invited us in to see her husband and brother. They were in a small room, used as a cell. This man was a friend at the compound and had been very kind to Miss Vaughan and Miss Cold.

When the war started and after the exiling of the Armenians, Miss Vaughan, the former missionary, was there alone after the first two

---

63. There is at this point in the typewritten manuscript a hand-written note—a clarification in the margin—that reads, "This man was only in Hadjin to secure help. He had come in the interest of the people of the town."

years. They and some of the Turkish women of Hadjin were very good to Miss Vaughan and our girls.

He naturally was glad to see Miss Cold, but was so sad. He did not understand his fate and he said he had never been in sympathy with the cruelty practiced on the Armenians. He had even given part of his house to refugee Armenians.

The other man was horribly rebellious. He was ready for anything to have revenge, if he ever got away from the building.

Things were much worse than we had expected to find them. The cruelty practiced upon the Turks, of course, was similar to what the Armenians had suffered in the last four years. But, oh, how badly we felt that it was only loaned these lawless men. And in return the innocent Armenians must suffer and perhaps our little folks and teachers.

As we were returning a Turkish woman followed us and walked with us to our home. Miss Cold kept her for the night. We did not expect her to stay because of the difference of our creeds. But she acted like a person temporarily insane from her experience of the last few weeks. We had to keep her under the influence of bromide until morning.

The Armenians had for years suffered the cruelty of the Turks. Now the condition was just the reverse for a short time, and the Turks did not understand.

Serious threats were made and Miss Cold's life was threatened because of her action.[64] Those poor people did not realize that she had knowingly gone in the interest of the people of Hadjin. She knew the outcome. The volunteer soldiers accused her of being pro-Turkish. The Armenians do not have a truer friend than Miss Cold.

The conditions were so pitiful and the sights which we witnessed were so terrible that we were unable to eat our supper that evening. It was utterly impossible for us to sleep that night because, when we closed our eyes, things would come before us until it was simply awful. It is beyond my power to describe that night.

Saturday, March 27th, was indeed a busy day. Miss Cold, Miss Clark, and I spent the greater part of the day in the sitting room. Some

---

64. The threats were coming from Armenians, or Armenian sympathizers, and it appears from the rest of the paragraph that these were *fedayees*. That such threats would have come from the Armenians of Hadjin seems unlikely, given Edith Cold's history with the community.

of the city people called and made excuses for their deeds at the Government building, saying that it was nothing compared to the experience which they had to suffer at the hands of the Turks. God would look at it in that light. It was true that they had suffered beyond all human reason. But whether God would look at it in that light was not for them to say.

Others came to us, saying they were sorry that we should find such terrible conditions and warning Miss Cold against any more visits. They told her that they understood her act and thanked her for her interest in their behalf. For she is absolutely fearless when she knows that she is doing the right thing in the right faith.

Sunday, March the 28th, all of our children left the Sunday School to see an aeroplane. About two weeks before a letter had been dropped from the second aeroplane that flew over Hadjin and created quite a little excitement. They said the aeroplane would make the landing if a place was prepared for it. A field was made ready for the Armenians on Mr. Eby's property but instead of landing they flew to an unusual height and unfortunately dropped another letter between Hadjin and the nearest Armenian village which was about six or eight hours ride by horseback from Hadjin. This letter fell into the hands of the Turks or Nationalists. It was the instructions which the French in Adana had given to the Armenians describing the code of signals they should use in emergency. It contained so many important facts which caused the Turks to mete out more severity to the Armenians. The letter was written in Armenian but it was taken to the nearby village and translated. The Armenians and the Turks had lived so closely that some of the Turks could speak Armenian just as fluently as the Armenians could speak Turkish. This letter was afterwards read in our sitting room by the Nationalists.

March the 29th, fighting occurred on the opposite side of the mountain in view of Mr. Eby's orphanage. Many wounded were given first aid there until they could be removed to the Armenian hospital in town. On Thursday, March 31st, a hard attack occurred on the mountain, the Turks gaining ground. Our women helpers were unable to reach the compound that morning. The garden was just ready to seed. We Americans and two native women helpers planted the seeds. In a few days these women were only allowed to be seen when it was absolutely necessary and we had to look after the garden, for we must have food for our children. Onions are one of the staple foods in the East.

On April the 1st, the Armenians driven from the mountains fought from Mr. Eby's property thus making it no longer safe for the children. The Turks were in full view of our compound. Previous to this the fighting had been from the opposite side of the mountain from us. For two weeks Miss Clark had taken her road bed and slept in the hall of the clinic building outside the compound wall where the girl orphans lived, for when the firing started the house mother was afraid to stay there alone.

On April the second, because of the near approach of the Turks, Miss Clark and Miss Cold decided to bring our children in from the clinic building outside the wall into the compound enclosure. With the crowded conditions, Miss Cold could not continue the studies. In the evening, the Mennonite Missionaries, their workers and children, must be brought into our compound as theirs was no longer safe. They had been under fire one week longer than we had. On account of the dangerous conditions they must make the trip at night. The Armenians took as their headquarters Mr. Eby's home, digging their trenches in the vineyard. On April the third, there was heavy fighting all morning. Up until this time, our flag had not been floated over our buildings. It was decided best to let the Turks know it was American property. By four in the afternoon the Nationalists were so near we could see plainly the Turkish flag which was placed on the mountains surrounding our compound.

Late in the afternoon, Miss Cold and Miss Clark thought it best to visit the boys' orphanage. The boys were then occupying the upper part of the factory. It was down under a hill and buildings surrounded and protected it from the Nationalists' fire. At first Miss Cold and Miss Clark could not decide whether it was safer to leave them in their present quarters or bring them to the school. I was preparing to go down to the Armenian hospital where I was to live until after the siege was over for the Medical Staff and the patients were alarmed and felt themselves unsafe unless they had our good old flag floating over the building and an American citizen living with them. I had been going down to the hospital for two hours every morning to help the wounded. This building which the Armenians were using as a hospital belonged to the

American board. When Miss Cold and Miss Clark arrived, our little boys and the overseer of the factory were with their teacher holding a prayer meeting. These two men were consecrated Christian men. Miss Cold said she had never attended a meeting like it before.

It was decided to bring our boys to the school for the section which had been occupied but two hours before was now deserted, and the hospital also, thus leaving our boys alone. The families who had sick and wounded in the hospital took them home for they were sure that every Armenian would be massacred that night and they said they all wanted to die together. When Miss Cold returned to the compound she said the hospital was a thing of the past. We had our supper and while we were at the table many families came and inquired if they could come to our compound. We only had room for our workers and Miss Cold told them that they were welcome to our clinic building just outside the wall. We were advised not to take the men into the compound. Only those who were employed by us could come in. But after dark several families came in until we had about three hundred fifteen. This meant that we were responsible for most of the food because they could not bring theirs with them as they had such short warning.

It was about twelve-thirty a.m., April the fourth. I had never seen a more beautiful night. It was full moon and as light as day. I heard someone pounding on the gate and started from my room. As I reached the bottom of the steps, I was met by Mr. Eby. We walked to the gate together. Miss Cold and Miss Clark had not heard them for they had a hard tiresome day. They[65] insisted on having the Turkish girls and wanted to see Miss Cold. We told them that it was night and Miss Cold was sleeping. However, it was necessary for us to waken her before the interview was over. She sent word that they should bring a letter in the morning from the *Commacum*[66] which is their highest official, similar to our mayor, before she would consider giving the children up, but would not do so until she received such a letter. She felt sure that

---

65. Though the "they" in this sentence is unspecified, it would seem, logically, to be Turks asking for Turkish girls, which perhaps complicates the question of motive. Although the tacit implication is that the men mean to take the girls for no good purpose, at the risk of sounding naïve, it is also possible that they might have been trying to take their own children back.

66. The word *commacum* here seems to refer to someone higher up in their military command, whereas Mary uses it earlier to refer to a mayor or civic leader in the town.

the letter would never come because the *Commacum* had not sent them at that hour. Had Miss Cold not shown the great wisdom which she did, the result might have been different. As it was, the Turks knew:[67] we did not know how they had heard, whether from spies or not.

April 4th, it was Sunday morning. The Turks started a terrible firing on our building and Miss Cold went out to investigate the cause and found they were firing on a father of one of the children who had followed his aunt into our compound the night before. He had come for his child. Miss Cold told him he would have to hide until dark. This was about nine in the morning and he hid all day and at dark the child was sent out to him. But we had occasional attacks all day in the direction of our compound.

April 5th, firing started on our compound about five and continued until ten in the morning. At first, Miss Cold was not sure the attack was intended for us. So she found it necessary to go over to the Martin house, a house belonging to our compound, and just escaped being wounded. The young girl who was one of our schoolgirls who followed her and whose business it was to look after certain rooms in that house was badly wounded in the leg. The Nationalists had been told that we had fifty volunteer soldiers in our school. When they realized the attack was not answered they put up the white flag and Miss Cold and Mr. Eby went out to meet them. Miss Cold first sent word to Miss Clark to make ready our sitting room, for it would be necessary to bring them in to make terms.

Miss Clark went into all that commotion as only she knew how, for every Armenian in our house expected to be massacred that morning and thought the only haven of safety was our sitting room. She and Miss Brademons, with the help of two native teachers, quieted that awful panic. For if any of you are ever with over three hundred people who are sure they will be massacred, you will realize the scene. All Armenians face the horrors of massacre from the cradle. The children tell you about it. That is what they have faced for years. The Turks say the guns are too good for the Christian dogs. The body is hacked with knives until some vital organ is reached and death relieves the suffer-

---

67. Presumably what they knew was that the relief workers were providing shelter to Turks, as well as to Armenians.

ing. I was unable to give any assistance, for near our sitting room door was a woman in a dead faint in her endeavor to reach a place of safety, she losing a husband and child in exile. She herself being one of twenty children, during exile she had many harrowing experiences, the last one being the following:

> At daybreak one morning an Arab called her out and all her jewels were taken. An Armenian at marriage is given what is known as her dowry which is always very precious to her. Then the Arab placed a Turkish coffee cup on her head and shot it off, telling her if she moved he would certainly kill her. She, of course, was too terror-stricken to move, and he a good shot. Next morning, he sent her away from the village with a company. When the English sent her back to Hadjin they asked her to give the Arab's name and, although she knew, she said she had suffered much, but would never tell the name of her deliverer.

After our family was safely hidden, Mr. Eby and Miss Cold escorted these creatures into our sitting room, for one could hardly call them men. I cannot describe their looks. I hope never to see fiercer looking ones again. One of them asked Miss Cold for our arms. We had one gun which was always carried on a village trip. You never travel in Turkey without protection of arms. Miss Cold said she would surrender that gun under one condition: that it was returned to her immediately, that we were without ammunition. This they promised after they had examined it carefully. They came in groups of two and stayed a short time, making six altogether. The last one being next in rank to Dogan Bey, Commanding General in Cilicia for Mustafa Kemmel, the Nationalists' leader.

They took as their headquarters the Armenian parsonage just outside our compound, demanding our cooking utensils and asking for sugar, salt, or coffee, promising a three-fold return which was never fulfilled. One time they asked for our coffee roaster, for they wished to roast their own coffee, but insisted on having our utensils, telling Miss Cold the commander preferred their roasting of coffee. Miss Cold said it was for lack of trust, thinking we might poison them. She made them understand our words were good and after that we, or our two Armenian helpers, roasted the coffee. It was a protection for us for borrowed articles were seldom returned and we dare not refuse them.

Things went fairly smooth for a few days. There is a saying that where there is not a desert where a Turk goes, he will soon make one, so this work began. They destroyed our beautiful valley by chopping out the tops of the lovely trees. Breaking into our clinic building, stealing what was loose at both ends and sometimes things which were not, but they found a way to loosen them, carrying the stash up the mountain side for their commander's camp, even destroying the house which was to house them until their departure. When they first surrounded Hadjin, they expected to take the city in a week's time. Being a burned city, the Armenians were able to dig deep trenches and cover their roads and mine their city and it was not easy to take for them.

Thursday, April 8th, they demanded the names of everyone in the school. After a conference of we six Americans [sic] and our Armenian helpers for the compound, we decided it best after much discussion not to give the information, Miss Cold saying it was something we need to pray over. We sent them word that at present we were unable to furnish the information. Up until now, our Turkish friends had never demanded it. Friday afternoon, April ninth, we were given one-half hour to furnish the paper asked for the day previous. Saturday morning about seven-thirty Miss Clark had an occasion to go out in the yard and these wild men were surrounding our compound. A few were on the inside and large numbers outside. Miss Clark called Miss Cold and she and Mr. Eby went out to the gate near the well and there they stood for two hours trying to bring those men to some agreement. And just outside that wall were three men sitting on the bank with their guns leveled at them, just waiting the signal from their commanders to fire.

After the end of that time, the house was searched and our family counted. Mrs. Eby and Mrs. Cold arranging them in the girls' dining room where they did not show off very well. Six men did the searching, but they all made a rush to accompany their leaders but one of them turned and said, "As you love God and the prophet Mohammed, stay where you are." Mr. Eby had to accompany the searchers. They were searching for the fifty volunteer soldiers they thought were hidden in our compound. Miss Brademons speaking Turkish, stayed out with

Miss Clark and I to keep these men out of the compound, but they soon found their amusement by destroying the surrounding Armenian property. One Turk entertained Miss Brademons while Miss Clark and I just looked on at the awful destruction taking place, unable to stop it.

April 11th was Easter Sunday. We were unable to have our Easter celebration, although an appropriate program had been prepared for that day. The native people held a prayer service in the girls' dining room. On Wednesday, April 14th, the Turks asked for a conference with the Americans, asking Miss Cold and Mr. Eby to act as their representative to the people of Hadjin. Their terms were that Armenians were asked to give up their arms and place them in a station, let the Nationalists go through Hadjin unharmed, and protect the Turks in their midst. There had been a report reach the Nationalist forces that all Turks in Hadjin had been killed. Some Moselems, after the town was surrounded, had escaped from Hadjin and joined the Nationalist forces. They told many conflicting stories of the treatment they received; unfortunately some were true, others false. The terms of peace would be decided by the truth of this report. The Turks sent word this was a last opportunity, after all this, all would be decided at the point of the gun.

On April 15th, Thursday evening, Miss Cold and Mr. Eby told the teachers and helpers what she and Mr. Eby had been asked to do in the morning, asking them to pray. On April 16th, a five-hour armistice was declared. Mr. Eby and Miss Cold left the compound about nine o'clock in the morning, Miss Cold carrying the American flag and Mr. Eby, the white flag. Three Nationalist leaders came down to escort them to the end of the Nationalists' trenches. The Armenian trenches and the Nationalist trenches were only a short distance apart and located on our road. When they reached the end of the Nationalists' line, the Armenians took them into Hadjin to the Armenian schoolhouse. They found some of our Armenian friends better off than they had hoped for. Some had died from the fire and others from disease taken. Many of the Turks had been housed in the Armenian Protestant church and were killed by the fire from some of the attacks which had taken place in Hadjin. Mr. Eby and Miss Cold did not persuade them to surrender, not wishing to take the responsibility, just stated facts; hearing them, they refused, saying they would rather die at the point of the gun than be massacred. This refusal came from the men in control of the government. Many citizens of Hadjin wished to risk the massacre to the awful attacks which would follow. They were not allowed to express their opinion, only to the Americans, and we could not get them to a place of safety.

What a suspense those five hours were at our compound. The children, and even some of the older ones, were so happy about Miss Cold and Mr. Eby going that they thought they could now go and stand just in front of the windows, in some instances taking down the unbleached curtains which Miss Clark had tacked up at the beginning of the siege to protect them from view of the men surrounding us. I wish some of our American people could have seen them. It fails me to give a description of the Nationalist troops. Those children and especially our Hadjin home girls had great confidence in Miss Cold's ability to adjust the trouble, Mr. Eby's people feeling much the same way. At the end of four hours, they returned.

A committee of Nationalists called at the end of five hours for the report. The only favorable news was that the Moselems were not all dead, but were distributed in some of the homes of the Armenians. We were sorry for the refusal but not surprised at the lack of trust on the part of the Armenians, their faith had been so often shattered before by false promises. The Armenians had discovered a rock in Hadjin which, from drainage of the city and a constant flow of water, had formed a chemical action and by pieces they ground it into powder and by putting some other chemical with it, they were able to make their gun powder. In this way they had ammunition for a long time (to July 27, 1921).

Saturday night, April 17th, an awful attack followed. Our poor little children; I wish you could have gone into our dormitory with me at night, my room being next. I made frequent visits to comfort the little ones. They felt safer when we were near. You would have found the smallest ones huddled together, but the older ones would have been either praying or weeping for those in the city. It was indeed a pitiful sight and the awful war cry of the Turk calling on God for help. It was also horrible for those poor children after the exile many of them had experienced. Our small orphans had been up to this time sleeping down in the kindergarten with an American always present. Miss Cold and Miss Clark relieved each other the first week, each taking half the night. Then the second week, Miss Brademons and Mrs. Eby each took a whole night's watch. It became necessary to move our children up to the already crowded dormitory, making them comfortable on the floor.

The Turks got an idea, too, that we had a covered road to Hadjin. Miss Clark had a lantern which was used in the kindergarten. It was not burned when the children were all right and sleeping. The Turks, not knowing the circumstances, thought it a signal to the Armenians. Then one night while Miss Brademons was sleeping with the children, they broke into the room next to the kindergarten and stole all contents of the room. Our food supply was greatly reduced.

Our chief diet was rice, dried beans, and onions. The children were reduced to wheat diet, we just being able as the time wore on to give them bread as a noonday meal. But if you could have seen those children, willing for anything, just for the protection of the Americans; it was indeed pathetic. For a time, Miss Clark had no Crisco or butter. Eggs must be used for one of our little girls who was ill. The milk was used for two babies. The canned milk was long since gone. Miss Clark had a small can of powdered milk which one of our relief workers had given her. The worker was stationed in Constantinople and, when she found Miss Clark was going into the interior, she thought she might have need of it. This was used very sparingly, but as time wore on and the Nationalists decided we were neutral, they would bring us small presents of cheese or butter or *uhort*, a food prepared with milk and artificially soured, resembling our sour milk. But if these presents were at all suitable, Miss Clark would always see that they were given to our sick children. After the Turks had been particularly troublesome and if they were at all repentant, they would bring you a present. Up until February, we had good wholesome food, partly provided by the Near East Relief and partly by the American Mission Board.[68] The food provided by the Board was native food.

About April the 30th, Enver Bey, the machine gunner, not being well, came to the compound from the mountains for medicine and while waiting for medicine entertained Miss Cold in the garden asking why we did not have a man to plant the garden, when he knew very well that because of them we must keep all the men hidden. While I was preparing the medicine he had our Kurdish shepherd dig up a bed

---

68. This small detail reflects the ongoing American humanitarian support in the midst of the Nationalist offensive.

and he planted the beans to show Miss Cold how. It was indeed a difficult matter for Miss Cold to plant and make that garden for sometimes it would turn into a place to entertain the men surrounding us. Many times she would entertain three or four at a time. We Americans were compelled to plant and care for the garden after April because the Armenians must be kept hidden and, as the summer was coming, a purely wheat diet was too heavy for our children. They must have green vegetables. We planted a large number of onions which provided some green. We often planted that garden when it seemed foolhardy to stay and yet we dared not leave and let them know we have the least fear. Sometime about the third week of April, Enver Bey sent a message down to know if he might come down to the compound and stay until he was well. Although Miss Cold felt it would make my work heavy, she also felt if he recovered, it would be the means of saving our children.

In April, Miss Cold had organized the children in a kind of progressive Sunday School, using our sitting room and the teachers' sitting room as the classrooms. After closing the day school, the children had very little to occupy their minds but the devastation of the Turks until Miss Cold, with the cooperation of the teachers, organized to vary the weekday classes. Sunday, up until this time, was a very trying day. We had to remind the children continually to keep quiet. They must not be seen during the day. In the evening Miss Cold would stay with them until bedtime, telling them stories.

We had just finished our morning medical work among our children when one of them came running to me saying, "Miss Super, a boy has been shot." I started toward the valley where I met the boy with some of his companions. He had been down in the valley minding the cow and if he had stayed in the shelter of the rocks he would have been safe. Just a short distance away was a lovely spring and he crawled on his hands and knees to get a drink. The Turks crossed the valley that way often. The Armenians saw him and thinking he was a Turk shot him. He did not know how badly he was wounded, saying his only thought was to get me. He crawled up the hill and when he reached the gate he saw how badly he was hurt. We had an Armenian doctor and druggist in hiding in our school and he insisted on amputating the hand but we had no facilities for an operation of that kind and then it was not necessary. We dressed his wounds and he was carried to my room which, ever since the siege, had been used as a hospital room. Any people or children in the house were taken there. Sometimes, we had five or six patients. The porch just outside my door, which Miss Cold had fitted up as a sick room, was not long safe. While my room was used for the sick, Miss Cold and Miss Clark were sleeping in Miss Cold's office and if anyone had wished to play a game of observation, that would have been a splendid place.

After dinner, word was brought to Miss Cold that a boy was lost on the mountain. His little companion had returned without him. She started out to hunt for him with one of the Turks who had been in our first searching party (and what an awful man he was), but she made him believe that she trusted him and he said he would go as her protector. She went from mountain to mountain until she found the boy, but he was afraid to come from his hiding place. She asked him if he was shot and he said yes, but he was just frightened.

April 20th, the second house searching and counting of our children. Our efforts to bring about peace were unsuccessful and we always suffered the consequence.

The Mennonite missionary's little Kurdish boy whom Mr. Eby had found in a cave, almost starved to death, lay dead. He was such a dear little boy and they were so glad to see him improve, but the little boy could not stand the strain we were under and, from the time we were surrounded, he started to weaken. His fright from the first house searching was too much. He begged Mr. Eby just to give them a piece of bread and they would leave. He worried so the day Mr. Eby and Miss Cold went into Hadjin.

We had another little boy who had been in Aleppo district when the bombs were thrown and he had a heavy cold. The awful strain we were under told on him. He was sick in bed and while I was preparing his medicine he was taken out of bed and carried into the dining room where the counting was going on. I reported the matter to Miss Cold and she said, "I am sorry, but I am just as helpless as if my hands were tied." He was in the dining room three hours and when he returned, he was carried to my room. He had a congestive chill shortly after reaching my room. We did all we could for him, but he died.

April 22nd, we carried the body of the little boy who died out and placed it alongside the little Kurd boy on the mountainside. We felt very badly about it, for up until we lost our little Kurdish boy, we had not had a death in either orphanage. How thankful we were, when our children were taken, that they were free from suffering.

We hoped in some way we might be able to save our little ones until help would come. We knew the Americans were trying to reach us, for the Turks told us so. Mr. Eby always went out to the clinic building to see that my instructions for administering the medicines were carried out for the Turkish servant.[69] He was sick two weeks and afterward stayed down with us to protect us from the wild hordes of men surrounding us.

The Nationalist forces were composed of seven leaders of robber bands, each man was supposed to have at his command one hundred men. The Turkish servant was very grateful for the care we had given him but owing to his protection of us we were compelled to grant any request he might make. These requests were very frequent and he would demand entertainment at any hour that suited his convenience. However, we were willing to do anything that would save our little ones.

Saturday, May 1st, the Turkish Judge's daughter left the compound. Miss Cold had been tormented night and day with conferences from her relatives. Three of our workers would spend hours in the sitting room while the relatives were calling. Miss Cold also had to see that they were fed.

Miss Cold was unwilling to let the girl go as she had been placed in our school for protection at the request of her parents and some of the Armenians of Hadjin, one of them bringing her to the school. Miss Cold sent a letter up to Doghan Bey stating the circumstances. His answer was if the relatives wanted her, we were free from all responsibility. These men knowing what might happen to our girls were anxious to get her to a place of safety.

---

69. This phrase is an odd one, and it seems to refer (anew) to Enver Bey and his extended bout of dysentery, during which he apparently came close to dying. Indeed, this label is repeated in the next paragraph and there more clearly refers to him, and the fact that Mary and the others experienced him as a protector, albeit a demanding one. They hoped that Mary's nursing him would protect the children. It is especially poignant that she notes this just after relating the death of a particularly loved Kurdish orphan in their care.

About May 9th, a number of children were out in the court just outside the girls' kitchen door when a report of an airplane was heralded
through the company and what excitement it caused. Some of the men
who had been afraid to come out of their hiding places came out in
plain view. They were delighted for they thought help was surely nigh.
The teachers and older girls remained in hiding, for they knew the significance of it. It turned out to be only a large eagle flying very high in
the air.

The Turks were very troublesome that day. Early in the evening they
started to stone the windows, breaking them in the schoolroom which
was being used as a dormitory. They had killed the animals for food,
just leaving the offal lying outside our gate. It was difficult enough to
maintain sanitary conditions inside the wall for over three hundred people. Miss Cold would go out and watch the mountains, so the Turks
could not harm the boys while they cleaned the drains.

The experience of the day had been too much. After a conference,
we Americans decided to send a note up to the Commander. It was answered early Monday morning in this way. "Unless we Americans were
a little more careful, we and the whole school would get the punish-
ment waiting for Hadjin." Miss Cold and Mr. Eby sent the messenger
back with a message that they did not understand the note but would
be glad of an interview with Doghan Bey. He sent his regrets, saying
he was sorry but it was quite impossible for him to come and he would
not be able to receive them. Gehan Bey and Enver Bey had a conference with us, the former making the excuse he had signed the note
which his men had written without reading it. Whether that was a fact
or not, we were glad to have it patched up. After they have caused you
trouble and they repent, they send you a present. This one happened to
be nuts and cheese. This provided food for our large family. We could
buy any quantity we wished. They needed both clothing and money
and, in exchange for food, we would sell the unbleached muslin from
our Near East supplies.

The villagers by this time had nowhere to sell their produce and were
compelled to bring it down and sell to us, if they could reach us before
the Nationalists saw them.

At the suggestion of one of our teachers, we sent up a present
of Turkish pastry to the Commander and also invited him to come to

dinner. He refused our dinner, saying after the siege, if all went well, he would be glad to break bread with us, but now it was impossible. It is against Turkish etiquette to break bread with anyone whom in the future they might harm.

About this time, we had a visit from a notorious robber leader, Gissehduran, meaning "the hidden one," and several of his men. They came at one and stayed until about five in the afternoon. At the first sound of the cannon, they prepared to leave our compound. At the second, which was about five minutes apart, they left. What an afternoon for those present. Mrs. Eby was not feeling well and did not come over until suppertime. I was busy caring for some of the children who needed medical care.

When they were still there at 4:30 p.m., I thought I would better go and see if I could be of any assistance. Miss Clark heard me entering Miss Cold's office. She came out and told me of their experience and asked me to pray that they might leave. All afternoon they had entertained them with the victrola playing our National music until they were finished and those present feeling they never wished to hear them again, never being sure of their next move. They were all dressed in the regalia belonging to a robber band leader of Turkey and his followers. I feel that no description I might make could possibly describe the afternoon of those present. The men were in the habit of coming to hear our victrola before. It seemed to be a source of amusement and a favorite pastime, but we were not anxious to have such distinguished visitors again. [70]

We were in the garden the next morning when the visitor of the previous afternoon came to call on me. We left the garden immediately as Miss Cold did not wish to entertain him there. He had asked frequently to see the "Doctor," for that was the title I received in Turkey. Nursing is not considered much of a profession in Turkey. We treated him as

---

70. Blanche Eby's description of the visit of "Gizik Douran and his wild band" is, in comparison with Mary's minimalist and sarcastic account of "distinguished visitors," a paradigm of titillating sensationalism and romantic projection: "Gizik Douran . . . possessed a certain hypnotic attraction, and cast about him a powerful influence. The Americans felt this fascination, and watched him with mingled feelings of curiosity and wonder. How could a heart become so brutal, so depraved, that robbery, murder, and the most horrible atrocities could be enacted without a single pang of conscience?" (Eby, *At the Mercy*, 190). Such comparisons remind us of the difficulties inherent in using memoirs as historical sources.

quickly as possible and gave him enough medicine so he would not return. After his visit, we lost one of our horses, making it necessary for a watch at night, the workers dividing the night into three-hour watches.

After that time, the compound was never without a guard, for the teachers divided the night into two-hour watches, two teachers in the school and two in the Martin House. After our little boy was lost on the mountain, we [came up with] a better plan [than] to send our flock out to the village: just keeping a cow and calf to have a little milk for several of our children.

One evening, the little boy who was lost on the mountain was taken out by one of the Turks to finish stealing the lumber left by the Turks during the first house searching. The Turks had destroyed the Armenian property and carried the lumber up the mountain. They had to leave all lumber which would endanger their lives. They built their officers' quarters by stealing other people's property. After [their] taking our little boy, one of the teachers called Miss Cold. She called the boy. Up until that time, he had been so frightened but when he heard Miss Cold he turned to the Turks who were taking him off and said, "Don't you hear who's calling me?" The man left the child there on the mountain and departed.

May 11th, the Kurdish children were asked for.[71] One, Miss Vaughn, a former Missionary, had taken into the school shortly after the war was over. When she came, she was very sick with dysentery and one would not have thought her recovery possible. After she was well, she was like a little wild animal. The contrast between her life now and when she came to us was very great. If she saw one coming in one direction, she would go the opposite way. She grew happy and contented with us and wished to stay. We had great hopes for her future, thinking she might some day go back to her people and teach them there was something more to live for than war and bloodshed.

The other was a little girl that Mr. Eby found in a cave almost starved to death. She was a pitiful sight when found with nothing on her but a burlap bag for a covering and her body was covered with vermin.

---

71. Again, the Nationalists seem to be attempting to remove everyone but Armenians and Americans from the compound, perhaps before they attack the building. Unfortunately, Mary does not appear to have known, and therefore does not clarify their motives.

We did not give the children up as we could not part with our little girl whom we had over a year and one half. Mr. Eby had their child only a short time. She was bent and looked years older than she was when they first received her into the orphanage. We were so interested to see her improving. We sent word to the Commanding Officer. He sent word to keep our children, as the men had not been officially sent and that we would have no further trouble as the men demanding the children had been sent to another camp.

However, two days later, one of our little boys went out to water our donkey and as he was riding back to the house he was shot. He was the one the Turks had taken to steal the lumber and who had been lost on the mountain. He had been out on the mountain with the cow while Miss Cold sat out, watching the mountainside while the boys cleaned the drain. He chatted in child fashion and was so happy and carefree, gathering green almonds for two of the workers but Miss Cold was so grieved in spirit and said she just prayed for wisdom and guidance, for one who is familiar with the Turks as she was can usually tell when they mean mischief.

The Kurds who had demanded our little children did the shooting and stood at the gate to see what would happen. After Miss Cold reached the almost lifeless body, two shots were fired which were probably meant for her and his head was almost severed from the body. When I reached Miss Cold, life was extinct. Our situation was so grave that she sent immediately for Mr. Eby to call Enver Bey who had not returned to the mountains since his recovery.

After Enver Bey arrived, we noticed him making a move to his men to retreat, telling Mr. Eby later if he had not arrived when he did we might all have been killed. We wrapped the little boy in two unbleached muslin sheets and strapped him to a ladder for we had nothing better. We slipped it through a hole in the wall, the two little boys who were going to dig the grave taking it on the other side. We Americans had to be very careful going out that valley gate because we were in danger of the Armenian fire from the town and the Turkish fire from the mountain. After the grave was ready, which must be just outside the wall, Miss Cold, Miss Clark untied his little form from the ladder and Mr. Eby and I placed it on the grave, Mr. Eby just having a short burial service. This made an impression on the Nationalists looking on. They said "what merciful people we Americans are." They suggested we just throw the body outside the wall but that did not accord with our feelings.

After this, we kept our children entirely out of sight. We had been particularly careful of our older girls and young teachers ever since the siege because of the threats of the Turks, but now all our children were kept hidden. Miss Brademons and Miss Clark got the water for over three hundred people, taking some of the little girls out after dark to help carry it in. We could not let the Turks know that we were afraid of what they might do. Miss Clark and Miss Brademons were stoned out by the well while they were waiting for two little children who were to carry the supply of water for the next day. Miss Cold had placed large native water jars on one of the flat roofs where the children played. When the three of these jars were filled, we would have enough water to supply the company for one day. I had a similar experience while gathering onions.

All our work must be done in the dusk. While we were doing our evening chores, Miss Cold entertained our children with stories. They were not allowed to speak much above a whisper and if you have ever tried to hush the spirits of three hundred children, you can realize the constant strain. Mr. Eby usually spent the time at the gate, buying the produce from the villagers, they, coming in the evening after dark or very early in the morning. Besides this, sometimes they would call on our steward and buyer and Miss Cold or Mr. Eby were always present as they had made several threats to exile him, saying he was sending messages and using signals of the position of the Turks. It was only Miss Cold's tact that saved the situation. His family were intermarried with the Moslems and when the threats were too serious, she would just call on some of the friends who had known him from childhood and for several days we would not be troubled.

When we would thank our workers, teachers and girls for service they would say, "O, that is nothing to compare with what you are enduring for us." All our teachers, workers and girls were willing to stand by us in any way that would help. They were so grieved that we were doing the work which we were compelled to do after our little boy was killed. Miss Cold and Miss Clark would go out every morning to superintend the cleaning of the drain from the toilet. Miss Cold would show the little boys how to work, for we were compelled to use some of the smaller boys, and Miss Clark would watch the mountains for any Turkish spies who might send a stray shot.

Wednesday, May 19th, we had a message from Doghan Bey or the Commanding General of Cilicia, saying he would call that afternoon. We were very glad for the conference, for up to just a few weeks ago, we were not just sure that such a person existed. His call was to ask Miss Cold and Mr. Eby to go in to Hadjin and bring about a reconciliation between their forces and the Armenians, terms to be much the same as stated at the first, only asking the Armenians to come and hold a conference at our school. Mr. Eby was asked to go out and announce the night before on May 20th that such a conference was desired and to say that a day of armistice was declared.

He went out about nine o'clock with a Turkish escort, going to a place between the two forces where he was permitted to communicate with several Armenians who understood English. He told them of the desire of the Turks for a day of armistice and also that he and Miss Cold would be in the next morning.

May 21st, Armistice declared from five o'clock in the morning. Miss Cold and Mr. Eby started, Miss Cold carrying the American flag and Mr. Eby the white one. Although the city was familiar to both, they had to be escorted into Hadjin for now it was a strong city of defence. It was indeed a long hard day. They returned about 2 o'clock and Miss Cold was carrying a beautiful bunch of red poppies. When Enver Bey saw them, he said in Turkish, "O, that means bloodshed." Miss Cold did not know that there was any Turkish superstition connected with red poppies.

Miss Cold and Mr. Eby came back and stated their terms. Some of the terms were accepted and some were not. They returned to Hadjin a second time that day. After much discussion, Miss Cold and Mr. Eby finally prevailed on two Armenians to come back with them and hold a conference and see if in some way they might reach a peaceable conclusion.

Miss Cold, Mr. Eby and the two men started, and were outside the Armenian line of defence when a shot passed between them, not injuring anyone. It was probably a sharp shooter, but the two representatives from the Armenians fled back to their own city and the conference was called off. It was not definitely known who was responsible for breaking the armistice.

May 22nd, another day of armistice, Miss Cold and Mr. Eby going nine times into Hadjin in two days, but their efforts were fruitless. The Armenians said the only way they would consider a conference was for a tent to be placed on our road just between their lines of defence and the Turks said the only place they would consider was our school. The Armenians refused this, saying they were ready for any consequence, no matter what it might be.

The Armenians refused to treat for peace because of the robber bands composing the Turkish army. We suffered the consequence of the refusal by another house-searching party and counting of our children. For his appreciation of the efforts of our two workers, Doghan Bey sent down a valuable present.

The Turks were so sure of the surrender of the Armenians for they felt they were both out of food supplies and ammunition but they had enough to hold out for several weeks.

We had a visit from the Circassian Commission. They had come to establish a form of government in Hadjin and also asked for medical aid.

From this until the seventh of June, the men were unusually troublesome. It was getting very warm and the villagers' crops and herds were being neglected.

They were celebrating their fast.[72] From the new moon in May until the new moon in June they fasted and the most devout ones will not allow any food to touch their lips not even water. They eat after sundown and then in the morning they must eat before daybreak before you can tell a black thread from a white one. Three heralds must proclaim it from a large Turkish centre. The place for Hadjin was Adana. A telegram was sent declaring the fast over. The same thing was done in June after the three witnesses had seen the new moon. A three-day feast was declared. There was much made of the feast of Ramadan[73] and the poor villagers were getting very restless to get home to their villages to attend this feast.

---

72. Mary is referring to the Nationalists' observances of Ramadan.
73. See n. 39, above, regarding the dating of Ramadan in 1920.

We had in all about twenty-eight or thirty attacks. Our own horses, sheep, goats, and kids stolen and cows shot. We had everything that could possibly happen, happen to us.

My patients at the gate ranged from twenty to thirty a day for eye treatments, gun shot wounds, syphilis, scabies or itch, malaria, dysentery and numerous other troubles. Sometimes they would come with their heads and arms, or wherever they had been suffering pain, gashing themselves with knives to leave the bad blood out. Even if any bones are broken, the same treatment is used by them. I frequently had them visit the clinic during the summer and by asking a few questions found the reason for the disfigurement. Another interesting thing: they would frequently change our dressings returning the next day with a black bandage next the wound. When you would inquire why they changed our dressing, they would say, "O, I did not want to dirty the doctor bandage." Some dirty old rag, usually black, next to the wound and your dressing on top. Then you would have to explain that you could not heal that wound unless they left the dressing undisturbed.

At first we treated them at the little back gate which indeed was memorable, being used by commanders as well as villagers. It was in a valley and out by the well. What a little gate it was, everyone coming in had to fairly crawl though.

The Turks were not in danger of the Armenian fire, but about the middle of May, Enver Bey thought it best to know what the villagers were selling or exchanging for unbleached muslin and all their produce. Patients were forced to come down the mountain, which would mean they must pass their camp, and they would take anything they wished from them. We pitied the poor villagers as much as we did the Armenians for those poor people were oppressed to the limit.

Our two Turkish friends, Enver and Gevann, had been acting strangely. Two days before, a Kurdish woman and a boy had escaped and gone to one of the Turkish officers' camp, telling that some of our children had escaped, which was true. Eight had gone into the city when the armistice was declared, but we had not reported the matter because they had counted our children after their escape. They made much of the matter, saying we should have sent them word.

June 7th: another count of our children, making serious threats of exiling them. We had tried many times to get word to the Mission

station at Talas. We were finally given permission to send for an order
of medicine from Talas and Miss Cold was allowed to send a letter in
Turkish. She sent to Mr. Wingate, a missionary at that station,[74] but,
unfortunately, he was in America. The letter was received by two of
the N.E.R. workers, the Doctor saying he did not place any significance
to the letter, thinking it was some young worker trying to show off her
Turkish.

We knew when they sent back the medicine that the letter had not
passed through the older Missionary's hands and that they did not know
of our plight. This had been our last hope of communicating with the
Americans. We knew the Americans were trying to get in to us, as we
had a message from Miss Allen[75] asking if we need food or money. The
name did not reach us correctly and we had to answer that telegram
saying we were well. The American Board, N.E.R. and Admiral Bristol
were all working to get to us, but there was only one way and that
through Talas and none of them knew that way.

June 7th, all day the Turks had been very restless. Enver Bey had a
wall of defense put up on the clinic porch and a shade made of branches
and the Turkish flag placed there. The 8th, the Armenians were firing
on that building all day long. About midnight of June 8th, the Armenians made a sortie, taking the three most important outposts of the Nationalists. They were forced to retreat and what a wild night that was.
Children and people so frightened and by 2 a.m. they had gained our
compound, made a forcible entrance, and entered our school. What excitement in that compound. Those men acted like insane men.

They demanded our children and at first we did not know whether
it was the Turks or the Armenians. Miss Cold stood at the top of one
staircase and I at the other. Miss Brademons guarded her room door to
keep them from entering her room, [thereby] gaining entrance to our
part of the house. Miss Clark was in hiding with the two Turkish girls.
Mr. Eby was out in the yard trying to protect the Turk[76] who for weeks

---

74. No one with the name Wingate is listed in any sources I have consulted.
75. Mary may be referring to Edith Allen Todd of Flatbush, NY, who is listed in Vickrey,
Teamwork. She came over on the *Leviathan* and was placed in Tiflis. But in September
1919, Miss Allen married J. Edward Todd and returned to Constantinople to work in "the
Bible House" with her new husband. It's possible that in June 1920, she was still writing to
mission stations inquiring about their needs. Or, it may be another Miss Allen entirely.
76. Enver Bey.

past had shown great kindness to our compound and whom the Armenians captured in our woodshed. Mr. Eby had been out with Enver Bey until midnight. The Armenians demanded our children and when some of the older girls refused, saying that Miss Cold had not given permission, they said, "You are an Armenian," and pointed their guns at them.

They were all like crazy men and since March had faced starvation and massacre. At night, the Turks would taunt them with threats saying they had taken our girls and forcibly married them. It was too much for their already weakened bodies and minds. They did not investigate the situation but just made the wild rush on the 8th of June with just a handful of men. They thought they had done it for a kindness for us and their children, but it was the worst thing which could have happened and they acknowledged later in the day their mistake, saying if they had known that we were so comfortable, they would have stayed in the city.

Although our position was far from comfortable, we, for weeks, had protected their children. They did what Miss Cold and Mr. Eby had asked them not to do, but it was an awful thing to face starvation and know someone has wheat which would sustain life until help came if the French would send it. They took some of their children the morning of June 9th and in the evening all the others were compelled to go. Some of them refused to leave us. Teachers who had taught at the school for years, some of our girls who were eighteen and twenty years old and in the graduating class. Many of them had been in the school from the time they were four or six years old. We just had to compel them to go. It surely tore our hearts to part with those faithful children and teachers. The morning the Armenians entered, they took possession of our school. This was Tuesday, June 8th.

Wednesday, June 9th, we cleared out our bathroom for a refuge and we stayed here part of a day and a night. Miss Cold had asked the Armenians not to fire from our building. We had to allow the Turks to do it. After we had been driven to the shelter of the bathroom, they started to carry up stones to use as a barricade. We were helpless to prevent this. We had been advised by our government to be neutral and Miss Cold said, "O, the joy of being neutral."

Thursday, June 10th, we had not a place of safety left but the stairway. We stayed here until bullets were numerous. We were advised by the Armenians to enter a closet which had been used as a place for storing wheat, large bins being built in the closet. It was also a general storeroom. This was cleared out the best we could under the circumstances. It was about ten feet by ten feet with steps going through the centre, the only means of ventilation being a grating in the floor above. What made it more difficult—in the kitchen above us was the pet horse which had been badly wounded and we had brought him into the girls' kitchen to dress his wounds and we could not get him out into the stable. With this horse above us and the dead bodies of men and animals on the outside, we had plenty of flies. We carried our mattresses and placed them on the floor. My two associates and myself at our school using a box which was just about half long enough and far from comfortable. Here we lived on nuts and tea. We only ventured out of our hiding place to get water and feed what animals were left of our stock. This must be done very early in the morning or after dark.

Then the wounded Armenians must be cared for. This was rather difficult, for most of our supplies had been carried into the town. Our last patient was a man with his radical artery severed. Nothing was left but a few horse sutures which were absolutely useless. I applied a two hemostal that I fortunately had carried into our closet and bandaged up the arm, keeping him a short time until we were sure the flow had ceased. We sent him to the druggist in the town for we could not keep him.[77] The Armenians were retreating and the Turks surrounding us again. The three days our building was bombarded, we were miraculously protected by our Heavenly Father.

At about 3 p.m. on June 11th, we were sitting at the door of the closet and those poor Armenians ran up and down the steps like caged rats. After a short time, they found a hiding place. There was an awful voice of an Armenian leader of a robber band who was trying to locate his superior officer. At midnight on June 11th, they left us. After they had all departed, we closed our closet door, just leaving it a crack and put our flag of surrender, a white flag, along with the American flag, over our closet door. We did not know whether the Turks would make a rush into our building that night or not. We waited until four a.m.,

---

77. See the Introduction, above, for an analysis comparing this passage with its parallel account in Blanche Eby's memoir. It is a pronounced example of Mary's understated style and selective narration.

June 12th. Miss Cold, Mr. Eby and I went up and put the white flag and
the American flag out the girls' dormitory window. Miss Cold called
out the window—"Friends, the Armenians are gone. There are six
Americans and two Turkish girls." They answered our call with three
signal shots. The awful destruction of our school was indeed pitiful.

We tried to clean up our girls' dining room which was a large room
just below our hiding place. We felt we must get where we could have
some ventilation. Then our closet, and indeed the whole place, was full
of flies from the stench of the dead bodies of both animals and men on
the outside. Stains of blood where men had met their death in our building. We heard occasional shooting during the day and it was indeed a
long day. At times, we found it necessary to return to our closet, but
still thinking we might use our dining room as a sleeping apartment
that night, dividing the night into two-hour watches. Mr. and Mrs. Eby
took the first watch, but as they were returning to their cots, Mrs. Eby
felt convinced she saw a man passing the window. In the darkness, we
had to cross the room and crawl up those steps again to our hiding place,
waiting until morning. Miss Cold and Miss Clark took the last watch.
At four, it was daylight and they started to draw our supply of water
for the day from the cistern.

June 13th about six o'clock, we heard the Nationalists calling and
Miss Cold and Mr. Eby went out to meet them. After much discussion,
they decided to enter our compound and some of their leaders searched
our building, insisting on Miss Cold and Mr. Eby going first. They went
out and gave the word that we were there with only two Turkish girls.
In a short time, our yard was filled with 30 or 40 of these lawless men,
ready for any destruction and—we were told after we had reached a
place of safety—coming with the intention of killing us Americans;
thinking we had broken our neutrality.

One of their first questions was, "Have you any Armenians present?"
Miss Cold answered, "No." They said, "It is well you have not." It was
only Enver Bey, dashing into the compound as he did, that saved the
situation. They had prepared an oil bomb to throw into our building and
burn us in it. He was the instrument God used to save us for he stayed
them from their wish of destruction, asking them to wait until morning.
He gave us two hours to leave the building. The men became uncon-
trollable and the time was shortened to less than an hour. We were told

we might carry hand baggage. We were compelled to make our toilet in our rooms with men stealing our personal belongings.

Enver Bey opened the house where all the Near East Relief goods were stored. These men were allowed to pillage the Martin House and afterward Enver Bey set the building on fire to safeguard our lives. While they were waiting the destruction of that burning building, Enver Bey took us out past the almost complete wreck and rapid firing from the Armenians and the answering fire of the Turks, which started when the former saw our building burning. Over dead men's bodies that had lain for days. The climb up the mountain was extremely difficult and hazardous and yet it had its humorous side. Enver Bey carried Mr. Eby's shoes, but not for Mr. Eby. When we reached his camp, he sat down and put them on. Mr. Eby asked him if they were not a little short and he said, "Yes. I believe they are yours." And Mr. Eby said, "Yes. I believe they are."

Enver Bey asked Miss Cold to let him help her up the mountain. She was carrying her riding whip. Enver took one end and she took the other, but when he got to the top of the mountain, he had the whip. He had lost both a riding whip and shoes the night the Armenians had the sortie. Miss Clark's patent leather bag changed hands several times, but not for Miss Clark.[78]

It was about three miles up that mountain and down the opposite side. We were allowed to rest a few minutes in Enver Bey's camp. Then we were taken down the other side of the mountain. We walked Shar Road and after we had walked a distance of about half a mile, they decided they did not wish us to stay there. We just retraced our steps and added about half a mile more to our walk.

We were still accompanied by our two Turkish girls. At one-thirty, we were served with tea and that was the first we had eaten since seven-thirty the night previous. After much discussion, the Turks decided it was best for us not to stay at this camp. It was where all the ammunition

---

78. This humorous tone is mirrored in Blanche's account of the escape up over the mountain, but in her narrative, it is Mary who does something funny: "The Doctor Lady seemed to be having a harder struggle for breath than the others, and, in spite of their mutual misery and discomfort, they laughed when they got a good look at her and discovered the reason. Fearing that all she might carry with her would be stolen from her, the Doctor Lady had donned several suits of clothing, and under the weight of them all was laboriously threading her way up the heights" (Eby, *At the Mercy*, 248).

was stored. On the other side of the stream was an open field and a large tree which the Turks had left standing. Here they spread blankets on the ground (which resembled our Near East blankets). Probably they were those stolen from Mr. Eby's orphanage. He had forty orphans supported by the Near East Relief.

As we were sent from camp to camp, we saw many things which formerly belonged to the Americans. To reach this spot, we must cross over two sycamore trees which served as a bridge. About 2:30, they served us a dinner which perhaps under the circumstances would have tasted good, but when we thought of our little folks frightened and perhaps hungry, for Hadjin was ill-prepared to feed three hundred more, we felt as if every mouthful would choke us. After dinner, word came down from the Turkish officers' camp that the directors of the school and the Doctor (or myself) were wanted for a conference at the camp. Miss Cold, who seemed never to lack wisdom, said that we did not wish to be separated and that we were too tired after our walk up the mountain. She felt if they separated us, we would be exiled. They sent animals and an escort and we had a beautiful ride up the mountain just at sunset. We left grieved to think we were getting further away from our workers, teachers and children who had been so faithful all through the siege.

We had our supper about seven. We were the guests of the Nationalists at their camp. We four Americans [sic] and the two Turkish girls occupied one part of the tent and Mr. Eby and the officer, the other. Under no circumstances could we have a restful night for we slept on a board floor. Besides, there was a great deal of commotion around us. Many telephone calls and they were guarded in what they said for they did not wish those of our number who understood Turkish to gain their position.

It was a wild night, a heavy attack, the Turkish forces were weak and if the Armenians had only been reinforced, great things might have been accomplished. They were celebrating their religious holiday, many of them escaping from their forces and returning to their villages

June 14th, the Nationalists put up a tent for us to use during the day. Here we were entertained by any who wished to call. In the afternoon, we were taken out by our guide to survey the city and its destruction from the binocular, also to see the cannon which was to destroy those poor people. They, of course, were delighted with the progress, but we were far from interested. Miss Cold said it was indeed hard to see the instrument which was to destroy the lives of our people.

At sundown, Doghan Bey returned and asked Miss Cold for a statement of our position all through the siege. She stated how the Nationalists had promised us Americans and our children protection and how, on the 8th of June, their forces were weakened and they had let the Armenians make a forcible entrance into our school and take our children. This statement did not please the Nationalists, for they wanted the blame placed on the Armenians.

Some of our number thought that Miss Cold had made a mistake not blaming the Armenians, that we might have had a safer journey to Talas as their prisoners, if she had. Miss Cold was absolutely fearless, feeling she was pursuing the right course. She said the Armenians already had much to suffer and she would not add to it with a lie. She was in the country as a representative of the truth and she would pursue it at the cost of her life if that was what her statement meant.

June 15th, we were given Turkish escort of three Turkish officers, one holding about the same position as policeman holds in our country and the other two, members of the Nationalist army. One was known to the American missionaries at our compound, those who had been shown much kindness. We made the trip for the first day on the German Army mules, purchased by the Turks during the war. The first night, we were entertained at a Kurdish village in the mountain pass of the Anti Taurus mountains. We three Americans living at our compound and one of our escorts were entertained at the Head Chief's and what an interesting old place it was. The Mennonites and the other escorts were entertained at the house of the Chief next in rank, who lived just across the way.

Divisoun Effendi, or the Chief who entertained us, had been given the pass as his possession if he could keep it free of robber bands, which he had been able to do for the last twenty years, making it safe for travel. We left his village about 8 a.m. on June 16th. He provided our animals. Our next village was three-hours ride from here and we must have a fresh relay and these returned.

We were usually entertained at the house of the Chief Official of the village where we stopped. We managed very well until the morning of the third day, June 17th, when we reached a village at 10 o'clock in the morning. It had been a large Armenian town and very prosperous before the war. All the Armenians had been driven out and their homes burned, only those remaining who had adopted the Moslem faith. We had breakfast here and after breakfast we were invited to take a walk around the town. During the walk, we were told that we were not going to Talas that night, but were to be taken to a village and perhaps exiled.

Now this was just what our friends in Adana and Constantinople had feared, because the Turks were not anxious to have their position known. We really had an exciting morning at the House where we were being entertained. Two of our number were sick and we had to reach the Americans at Talas by night.

Miss Cold said to me, "You must insist on reaching the Americans by night." So I kept insisting to our guide, Miss Cold interpreting what I was saying, that for the good of our friends, we must reach Talas. The reason Miss Cold had to interpret my conversation to the Turk was they thought I was a Doctor and gave me that title. She felt my words would have more weight under those circumstances. The guide, who was a friend of Miss Cold, felt very sorry for the treatment we had been subjected to, so he promised her we should reach our friends by night.

He managed very well until one o'clock. We entered a village where a large company were going through their devotions. They left us sit along the stream for two hours. Each village, as we entered, was supposed to provide food for us. After waiting two hours and no animals nor food being provided, our Turkish guide, Hartin Effendi, used manual force, knocking two men down and slapping another along the side of his face until he cried like a baby. He gave them one half hour more to get us dinner and provide animals. At the end of that time, we were still waiting. He went in and set one of their homes on fire. They made a great fuss over the fire. The whole village were up in arms to have the fire put out. Horses were soon forthcoming and the fire was put out. Our dinner was brought and the three Mennonites ate the dinner but we did not because the surroundings were terribly dirty and we were not hungry and our guide did not, because he had had the trouble with the villagers.

We were sorry for the poor villagers but we were very glad to leave the village and start for Talas which we reached about seven o'clock.

We were indeed glad to reach Americans for we did not have road beds or blankets and the vermin in the East are considered a necessity.

You can imagine how we enjoyed a clean American home after our experiences. We arrived in Talas on the evening of the 17th of June and left on the morning of the 23rd of June in one of our two-ton trucks, arriving at Sivas at ten o'clock in the evening, after being stopped five times by the Nationalists to know our business and how much gasoline we carried.

We had a three day auto trip, arriving in Samsoun on June 26th. The three Mennonite missionaries, three transportation men and myself left Samsoun on the evening of June 28th. Miss Brademons and the three transportation men held passports but Mr. and Mrs. Eby and I had ours stolen by the Nationalists when they took our other possessions. Fortunately, Mr. and Mrs. Eby had the papers with the red seal which the Near East provide all workers or those traveling under the protection of the Committee as the Mennonite missionaries were. They were very official looking and served as a passport. They were signed by Dr. Mc-Callum.

I had nothing but a paper made out by the British High Commissioner of Samsoun because our American Consul was out of town. My paper stated I was on my way to Constantinople on business. When Mr. Eby showed my paper to the Turkish official he said, "That is our destroyer," and the British war vessel was not in the harbor and they would not allow the paper to be used as a passport. It was a dirty little Russian vessel, third class passenger using the deck as their stateroom and besides all this we had two dirty pet lambs on board, one belonging to the captain and the other to a Turkish woman passenger. This was the only place we could sit.

Our staterooms were small, stuffy, and the berth so small that we were unable to stretch out full length. My berth had a broken spring and every kind of vermin one could mention. Just outside of our stateroom was a very sick man who moaned and groaned most of the time. We were three nights on board this dirty vessel, just arriving in Constantinople at sundown. All business offices were closed at this time of day, but it was the best we could do as traveling was extremely difficult in the East at that time and we could not wait for the Destroyer, there being too many in our party. The Destroyer was only used as a courtesy of our Government to women passengers, some of the officers of the crew giving up their staterooms for the convenience of the women. We received a hearty welcome from the Near East Office at Constantinople on our arrival. This was July 2nd. I was entertained at Headquarters.

On July 4th, Admiral Bristol and wife invited all Americans in Constantinople to the Embassy to a reception.

July 20th, we sailed. In our party was another Red Cross nurse and Y.W.C.A. worker and a young man of the Near East Relief who had given splendid service in Harpoot. We sailed on a Brazilian vessel being used by the French as a transport. Our fellow passengers were French officers, several being accompanied by their wives and children and four French Red Cross nurses. We stopped at Bone, a French and Arabic town on the north coast of Africa, for three days, this being a wine centre. We unloaded here five hundred empty wine barrels and five hundred Algerian soldiers.

At Bone, we were met with the cheerful news that the Itn was under orders to return to Constantinople and we would have to trans-ship for Marseilles, but in a few hours a telegram arrived saying the last order was to go on to Algeria, where the Itn would lay in dry dock a month for repairs or return in a few days to Constantinople. We had four days in Algeria which was an unexpected pleasure.

July 30th, we trans-shipped on the *Marshal Begeand* bound for Constantinople. This vessel was already crowded and just two of us secured berths, the others using steamer chairs. The company from the N.E.R. were offered the third class passengers' quarters or the deck, so they selected the latter as it was so hot in the hold.

August 2nd, we arrived in Marseilles. Our arrival was very impressive by the French National airs reaching us from the bugler. They were playing from the rocks in the harbor.

August 7th, we left Marseilles on the Roma, bound for New York. We came through the Strait of Gibralter about 7:30 one evening. It was rather a hazy evening, but we were close enough to get a good view of the rock.

We stopped a day and a half in Lisbon, Portugal. What an interesting old city from the harbor, but, oh, the poverty. The English High Commissioner who sat at our table said you could not even get a box of matches. We did secure a few postal cards. When we asked him how they made a living, he said they took in others' washing. They had changed its form of government eight times in six months. Royalists in prison, frequent revolution, armed soldiers wherever one might look.

We took our first steerage passengers, five hundred of them, bound for Providence, R.I. We were in the harbor a day and a night. Our next stop was at the Azore Islands. We were a day at Ponta del Gada, sightseeing. It was a lovely island with sulphur springs and glaciers resembling our Yellowstone Park. We had several hours sailing before reaching the second group of islands on Sunday morning.

August 15th at nine a.m.: the last group. At three in the afternoon, we took on several hundred steerage passengers at each of the groups of islands, most of them bound for Providence, R.I. The factories of New Bedford, Connecticut [sic] find the Portuguese very satisfactory help.

Our next stop was Providence, R.I. We were here a day and a half and received a very hearty welcome from the American Red Cross. In fact, all along the way, wherever we met the Red Cross, we were treated with courtesy and consideration.

We arrived at Providence, R.I. on August 22nd, leaving at noon of the 23rd and arriving at Brooklyn on August 24th. We called up the Near East Office and they advised us to go to the Albert Hotel. In the afternoon, we reported at the office of the Near East and we Red Cross nurses, to our office. At one o'clock on August 26th, we had a reception at the Aldine for a few of the office force and those returning on the Providence and our party. The honored guests were Dr. Barton[79] and Mr. Jaquith.

If you think of a Nation who has worshipped a man, or Mohammed the Prophet, for centuries, you have a picture of the Turks. The Prophet was born six hundred years after Christ and is considered by the Moslems the last and greatest Prophet. Mohammedans claim that the Koran, their book, was transmitted verbatim to him in the Arabic language. The Moslems believe in polygamy and in the use of the sword. Can you think why they should not degenerate, or any nation with such principles?

---

79. James L. Barton, foreign secretary of the American Board of Commissioners for Foreign Missions.

They are terribly superstitious. You never look at their babies unless they are sick and it is necessary. To just go along on the highway and look at a baby, they do not wish you to, unless you can say in Turkish a blessing. They think blue glass beads, which you see sewed on their clothing (even the animals have strings around their neck) will keep the curse of the Christian eye off their belongings. If you would buy at the pigeon Mosque in Constantinople a string of prayer beads, you would probably be given a little blue or green glass stone on which are inscribed Arabic characters known as the evil eye.

They have ninety-nine ways of calling on God.[80] I had a Sunday school class of thirteen fine young Armenian girls and I used to say, "Girls, the kindest thing we can do for them is to pray for them. They do not know our Savior." And I would quote Matthew 10:26 to them.[81] They would say, "Miss Super, I know, but it is hard to pray for people who have massacred your father in front of your eyes." I would tell them it was impossible for them, but Christ could so fill their lives that they would be able. And they did. Every one of those girls helped serve the Turks. My little helper washed bandages which were filled with vermin, for we were compelled to use them as many times as possible, for our supplies were exhausted. She did it without a murmur, and the only way it was discovered was when I went to wash those bandages myself and she said, "O, don't Miss Super, they are too dirty for you to touch." We soaked them with bichloride solution, but after that, Miss Cold had us bury them, as typhus can be carried by body lice. Others of them made pastry for Doghan Bey. Some of the women washed for Enver Bey and baked bread.

The Turks are inquiring the difference between our Book and theirs, many of them feeling Mohammed has failed them and they want to know how they can become American citizens, thinking that makes the difference between their lives and ours, not knowing it is the promise of attaining heaven that they need.

O, what a pitiful thing and what an awful war cry they had, calling

---

80. Mary is referring to *Al-Asma-Ul-Husna*, the beautiful names or attributes of God, reference to which may be found in the Qur'an, Surah 7:180.

81. "So have no fear of them; for nothing is covered up that will not be uncovered, and nothing secret that will not become known" (Matt. 10:26, New Revised Standard Version).

on God for help, while they were killing innocent men, women, and children.

One night, when they were having a very hard attack on the town and I was in with the children in the dormitory accompanied by one of our young teachers, she said, "Listen, Miss Super, they are calling on God, and don't you feel sorry for them?" And I said, "Yes. I do."

Appendixes

A Note on the Appendixes

T he historical documents collected in the appendixes reflect the sociopolitical context of the memoirs and the events narrated within them. They include American presidential letters, political declarations and manifestos, newspaper articles, fundraising posters, political cartoons, and papers pertaining to Mary Super and her fellow relief workers. I have also chosen to reproduce excerpts from the memoirs of Alice Clark and Blanche Eby that address larger historical questions. In the case of Alice, these are questions about lack of intervention on the part of the French and defensive measures on the part of the Armenians; in the case of Blanche, the earlier history of the deportations and exile of the Armenians is described through survivors' eyewitness stories.

The appendixes will help to edify the reader, frame some of the events that Mary narrates, and clarify some of the questions that arise within her narrative. In particular, the appended materials are organized to provide examples of discussions about foreign intervention—particularly American intervention—in the region during Mary's time there; the ways in which public opinion, philanthropy, and relief efforts were leveraged in the United States and the centrality of religious discourse to that process; and the history of Ottoman/Turkish repression and Armenian resistance and nationalism.

APPENDIX A

American Presidential Angst and Questions of Foreign Intervention

A.1: November 26, 1917. Letter to President Woodrow Wilson from Henry Morgenthau. *Library of Congress: The Papers of Henry Morgenthau Collection, Reel No. 8.*

A.2: May 11, 1918. Letter from Theodore Roosevelt to Cleveland Dodge. *The Letters of Theodore Roosevelt*, ed. Elting E. Morison. Cambridge, Mass.: Harvard University Press, 1954. Reproduced in *The Armenian Genocide and America's Outcry: A Compilation of U.S. Documents 1890-1923*. Washington D. C., Armenian Assembly of America, 1985.

A.3: September 18, 1919. Telegram from President Woodrow Wilson to Acting Secretary of State William Phillips. Reproduced in *The Armenian Genocide and America's Outcry: A Compilation of U.S. Documents 1890-1923*. Washington D. C., Armenian Assembly of America, 1985.

A.4: May 24, 1920. Special Message to Congress from President Woodrow Wilson. From *A Compilation of the Messages and Papers of the Presidents: Prepared Under the Direction of the Joint Committee on Printing of the House and Senate, Pursuant to an Act of the Fifty-Second Congress of the United States (With Additions and Encyclopedic Index by Private Enterprise), Volume XVIII.* New York: Bureau of National Literature, Inc. Reproduced in *The Armenian Genocide and America's Outcry: A Compilation of U.S. Documents 1890-1923*. Washington D. C., Armenian Assembly of America, 1985.

A.5: May 27, 1920. Message to the House of Representatives from President Woodrow Wilson. From *A Compilation of the Messages and Papers of the Presidents: Prepared Under the Direction of the Joint Committee on Printing of the House and Senate, Pursuant to an Act of the Fifty-Second Congress of the United States (With Additions and Encyclopedic Index by Private Enterprise), Volume XVIII*. New York: Bureau of National Literature, Inc. Reproduced in *The Armenian Genocide and America's Outcry: A Compilation of U.S. Documents 1890-1923*. Washington D. C., Armenian Assembly of America, 1985.

A.6: November 22, 1921. Letter to Secretary of State Charles E. Hughes from President Warren Harding. Reproduced in *The Armenian Genocide and America's Outcry: A Compilation of U.S. Documents 1890-1923*. Washington D. C., Armenian Assembly of America, 1985.

A.1

November 26, 1917
Letter to President Woodrow Wilson from Henry Morgenthau

In this letter, Morgenthau lays out his plan to "mould public opinion" in order to ensure public support of the war. Morgenthau sought to influence not only public opinion but also municipal elections in the interests of war. Provoked by anti-war sentiment among "Democrats, Independents and Socialists" in New York, Morgenthau proposed to Wilson to "concentrate the public mind" on "Germany's intrigue and perfidy," and on Turkey as "the cancer in the life of the world": "For in Turkey we see the evil spirit of Germany at its worst—culminating at last in the greatest crime of all ages, the horrible massacre of the helpless Armenians and Syrians."

November Twenty-Sixth, 1917.

My dear Mr. President:

You will recall that when I returned from Turkey in February, 1916, I was very much concerned and alarmed by the indifference displayed by the National Democratic Committee concerning the coming Presidential election.

I insisted that you permit me to resign my post and devote myself to the task of rousing the Democrats from their lethargy, and infusing enthusiasm amongst them for this campaign. I am prouder of my share in your re-election than any other service I have ever rendered.

At present I am again Cassandric in mind and want to sound an alarm as regards the coming Congressional election. It would be an irremediable calamity if you did not receive a thorough vindication of your splendid administration in the 1918 election.

Fortunately the Democratic Committee, George Creel and others are working faithfully. You are every day doing your Big Bit towards moulding public opinion. But many of our citizens are still opposed to the war, and their stand is largely based on ignorance of the causes, the scope and the results of the war.

My interest in the New York municipal election was not due to any personal affection for the candidates. It was entirely due to my devotion to good government and to my belief that the growing anti-war senti-ment in New York had to be fought as vigorously as possible. I ad-dressed a great many large and some small meetings, and mixed with Democrats, Independents and Socialists. I was greatly discouraged at the amount of outright opposition and the tremendous indifference to the war, as well as by the lack of enthusiasm among the mass of those who are supporting the war.

It has occurred to me that someone should undertake a very specific task which now presents itself to me as necessary. This task is to con-centrate the public mind upon certain facts leading up to the war with a view to rallying the indifferent and winning those who oppose us. The situation requires that the story of Germany's intrigue and perfidy be adequately set down in a way to be perfectly comprehended by our people. The premeditated and carefully organized effort to interfere in the government of almost every nation in the world, to plant discord between nations, the whole outrageous scheme to dominate Europe and even America —that is the side of Germany with which Americans are not yet fully acquainted.

It can easily be shown that Turkey was the cancer in the life of the world, and, not being properly treated, has now grown into the greater cancer of Central Europe. If the Turks have, for four hundred and fifty years, constantly endangered the peace of Europe, what will happen to the world if Germany and Turkey now assume the role of tyrant and troublemaker together?

The system of permeation through diplomatic agents and spies, which has marked the whole organization of Germany's foreign policy, is nowhere so evident as in Turkey and the Balkans.

I should like, with your approval and assistance, to undertake the preparation of this story on *a larger scale* than I have done in the en-closed articles.

I am considering writing a book in which I would lay bare, not only

Germany's permeation of Turkey and the Balkans, but that system as it appears in every country of the world. The German permeation of Turkey and the Balkans, their winning of Turkey and then Bulgaria, plus their destruction of Greece, placed the veritable keystone of their power on the Bosphorus. The peculiar facilities I had of informing myself upon this phase of the subject, seem to make it incumbent upon me to tell my story at this time. For in Turkey we see the evil spirit of Germany at its worst — culminating at last in the greatest crime of all ages, the horrible massacre of the helpless Armenians and Syrians. This particular detail of the story and Germany's abettance of the same, I feel positive will appeal to the mass of Americans in small towns and country districts as no other aspect of the war could, and convince them of the necessity of carrying the war to a victorious conclusion.

I have been informed that this book can be syndicated and published simultaneously over the whole country in the important daily newspapers, and in some of the larger agricultural publications. The book should be published early this summer and I would like your opinion as to the advisability of my giving the entire profits to a Congressional Campaign Committee: this Committee to undertake under the proper direction to assist all Congressional candidates of whose loyalty and support to the Administration, there can be no doubt.

We must win a victory for the war policy of the Government and every legitimate step or means should be utilized to accomplish it. I am anxious to hear whether my plan meets with your approval.

With kindest regards, I remain
Yours faithfully,

President Woodrow Wilson,
White House,
Washington, D.C.

A.2

May 11, 1918
Letter from Theodore Roosevelt to Cleveland Dodge

This excerpt from a letter, written almost a decade after Roosevelt left the presidency, advocates that the United States go to war with Turkey because of the Armenian massacres; otherwise all Wilson's talk of "making the world safe for democracy" (in his April 1917 appeal to Congress to declare war on Germany) is nothing more than "insincere claptrap."

Oyster Bay, May 11, 1918

To Cleveland Hoadley Dodge

… So far from "being of assistance to the Allied cause by keeping on nominal terms of friendliness with Bulgaria and Turkey," I am convinced we are of the very greatest damage to the Allied cause by so doing. Moreover, I feel that we are guilty of a peculiarly odious form of hypocrisy when we profess friendship for Armenia and the downtrodden races of Turkey, but don't go to war with Turkey. To allow the Turks to massacre the Americans and then solicit permission to help the survivors, and then to allege the fact that we are helping the survivors as a reason why we should not follow the only policy that will permanently put a stop to such massacres is both foolish and odious.

I have a most interesting letter on the subject from Einstein, formerly with our Embassy in Turkey. I will send it to you by George Perkins. Some suffering would be caused if we went to war with Turkey, just as some suffering was caused when we went to war with Germany. But the Americans now would suffer only as the English and French suffered three years ago, when their nations were doing their duty, and ours was shirking its duty. We have no business to expect the allies to do the fighting which alone will accomplish anything permanent while we play the utterly ignoble part of being neutral and hoping that somehow or other we can thereby both save our own skins and also accomplish something. The arguments advanced against our going to war with Turkey are on a par with those formerly advanced against our going to war with Germany and then with Austria; only they are not quite as good. The Armenian horror is an accomplished fact. Its occurrence was largely due to the policy of pacifism this nation has followed for the last four years. The presence of our missionaries, and our failure to go to war, did not prevent the Turks from massacring between half a million and a million Armenians, Syrians, Greeks and Jews—the overwhelming majority being Armenians. Our declaration of war now will certainly not do one one-hundredth part of the damage already done by our failure to go to war in the past; and it will enable us to render service of permanent value for the future, and incidentally to take another step in regaining our self-respect.

We should go to war because not to do so is really to s how bad faith towards our allies, and to help Germany; because the Armenian massacre was the greatest crime of the war, and failure to act against Turkey is to condone it; because the failure to deal radically with the Turkish horror means that all talk of guaranteeing the future peace of the world is mischievous nonsense and because when we now refuse to war with Turkey we show that our announcement that we meant "to make the world safe for democracy" was insincere claptrap.

A.3

September 18, 1919
Telegram from President Woodrow Wilson to
Acting Secretary of State William Phillips

This telegram from President Woodrow Wilson to Acting Secretary of State William Phillips asks him to approach Congress about sending troops to Armenia, and to possibly pursue joint military action with the French, just days after Turkish Nationalists had met at the Sivas Congress and as the Kemalists were centralizing resistance efforts.

TELEGRAM RECEIVED Plain

> Dun..., California
> Undated
> Recd. September 18th, 1919
> 1234...

Honorable William Phillips,
Acting Secretary of State,
Washington, D. C.

I would be pleased if you would get into communication with Senator Williams and through him with the appropriate committees of Congress with regard to our being authorized to send troops to Armenia. I am heartily in favor of such a course if the Congress will authorize it, but of course am still willing to defer to the French if they are sending a sufficient number or to join them if they are willing to accept joint military action and we get the authority of Congress.

WOODROW WILSON

A.4

May 24, 1920
Special Message to Congress from President Woodrow Wilson

In this excerpt, Wilson requests that the government of the United States "become the helpful friends and advisors" of the Armenian people; that is, that the Congress grant him executive power "to accept for the United States the mandate over Armenia." His request came in response to an invitation from the Council at San Remo. Note the pronounced rhetoric of Christian solidarity, also discussed in the introduction.

The White House, May 24, 1920

It is to this people and to their government that the hopes and earnest expectations of the struggling people of Armenia turn as they now emerge from a period of indescribable suffering and peril, and I hope that the Congress will think it wise to meet this hope and expectation with the utmost liberality. I know from unmistakable evidence given by responsible representatives of many peoples struggling toward independence and peaceful life again that the government of the United States is looked to with extraordinary trust and confidence, and I believe that it would do nothing less than arrest the hopeful processes of civilization if we were to refuse the request to become the helpful friends and advisors of such of these people as we may be authoritatively and formally requested to guide and assist.

I am conscious that I am urging upon the Congress a very critical choice, but I make the suggestion in the confidence that I am speaking in the spirit and in accordance with the wishes of the greatest of the Christian peoples. The sympathy for Armenia among our people has sprung from untainted consciences, pure Christian faith and an earnest desire to see Christian people everywhere succored in their time of suffering and lifted from their abject subjection and distress and enabled to stand upon their feet and take their place among the free nations of the world.

WOODROW WILSON

A.5

May 27, 1920
Message to the House of Representatives from
President Woodrow Wilson

In this message, Wilson refuses to sign a Resolution to repeal standing declarations of war against Germany and Austro-Hungary, because the Resolution to repeal contains no insistence upon, among other things, "the release of the Christian populations of the Ottoman Empire from the intolerable subjugation which they had for so many generations to endure . . ." Wilson frames the Resolution as unworthy of "the gallantry and honor of the United States," "the dignity of the United States," and "the very fundamental conditions of civilization."

The White House, May 27, 1920

To the House of Representatives: I return herewith, without my signature, House Joint Resolution 327, intended to repeal the Joint Resolution of April 6, 1917, declaring a state of war to exist between the United States and Germany, and the Joint Resolution of December 7, 1917, declaring a state of war to exist between the United States and the Austro-Hungarian Government, and to declare a state of peace. I have not felt at liberty to sign this joint resolution because I cannot bring myself to become party to an action which would place ineffaceable stain upon the gallantry and honor of the United States.

Notwithstanding the fact that upon our entrance into the war we professed to be seeking to assist in the maintenance of common interests, nothing is said in this resolution about the freedom of navigation upon the seas, or the reduction of armaments, or the vindication of the rights of Belgium, or the rectification of wrongs done to France, or the release of the Christian populations of the Ottoman Empire from the intolerable subjugation which they have had for so many generations to endure, or the establishment of an independent Polish State, or the continued maintenance of any kind of understanding among the great Powers of the world which would be calculated to prevent in the future such outrages as Germany attempted and in part consummated.

We have now, in effect, declared that we do not care to take any further risks or to assume any further responsibilities with regard to the freedom of nations or the sacredness of international obligations or the safety of independent peoples. Such a peace with Germany—a peace in which none of the essential interests which we had at heart when we entered the war is safeguarded—is, or ought to be, inconceivable, as inconsistent with the dignity of the United States, with the rights and liberties of her citizens, and with the very fundamental conditions of civilization.

I hope that in these statements I have sufficiently set forth the reasons why I have felt it incumbent upon me to withhold my signature.

WOODROW WILSON

A.6

November 21, 1921
Letter to Secretary of State Charles E. Hughes from
President Warren Harding

In this letter, Harding asks Secretary of State Charles Hughes to informally approach British Foreign Secretary Arthur James Balfour and French Prime Minister Aristide Briand about sending a warship "to an Armenian port on the Mediterranean" in order to "restrain the hands of assassins in that unfortunate land."

The White House, Washington
November 21, 1921

My dear Secretary Hughes:

   I am enclosing herewith a copy of an appeal presented to me today by a Committee of Americans who called on behalf of the Armenians in Cilicia. I had something to do with the inquiry into the Armenian situation during the latter part of my term in the senate, and I am disposed to think there is a good deal of ground for the gloomy view of the situation in Cilicia which is presented in this appeal. I am wondering if it would not be possible for you to speak informally concerning the matter with Mr. Balfour and Mr. Briand. I would not want the question intruded into the Conference program, but I can well believe it to be in thorough harmony with the spirit impelling us to inquire if an informal word can not be exchanged with these two delegates which will bring some assurance of safety to this dreadfully stricken people.

   When I was in the Senate I had the honor to recommend to the Executive the dispatch of a Navy vessel to the port of Batun on the Black

Sea. The purpose at that time was to enable a sufficient force of marines to be employed to keep open the railway from Batun to Erivan in order to guarantee the transmission of relief supplies and otherwise tranquilize the situation. If it is believed that a warship can be sent to an Armenian port on the Mediterranean I should have very little hesitancy in making such a suggestion on behalf of these stricken people. Surely there must be some way in which to utter the admonition of the five great powers to restrain the hands of assassins in that unfortunate land. If you would prefer me to personally broach the subject in an informal way to these spokesmen for Great Britain and France I will have no hesitancy in doing so, but I would much rather that the sympathetic inquiry be made by you.

Very truly yours,

Hon. Charles E. Hughes,
Secretary of State,
Washington, D. C.

APPENDIX B

Informing the American Public: Mobilizing and Maintaining Public Opinion

B.1: *The New York Times*, "Appeal to Turkey to Stop Massacres," April 28, 1915.

B.2: *The Washington Post*, "Crucified by Turks," April 29, 1915.

B.3: *The New York Times*, "800,000 Armenians Counted Destroyed," October 7, 1915.

B.4: *The New York Times*, "Aid for Armenians Blocked by Turkey," November 1, 1915.

B.5: *The New York Times*, "Million Armenians Killed or in Exile," December 15, 1915.

B.6: *The Christian Herald*, "God Save Armenia!" November 1, 1916.

B.7: *The New York Times*, "Armenian Tells of Death Pilgrimage," July 27, 1919.

B.8: *The Independent*, "Shall Armenia Perish?" by Henry Morgenthau, February 28, 1920.

B.9: Popular Media Images

B.9.a: American and British Relief Posters about Armenia, c. 1915, Histories and Narratives Collection, Armenian-Turkish Research Project, University of Minnesota Center for Holocaust and Genocide Studies. Online: http://chgs.umn.edu/histories/turkishArmenian/ (accessed January 24, 2009).

B.9.b: Editorial Cartoons of the Armenian Genocide, Histories and Narratives Collection, Armenian Genocide, University of Minnesota Center for Holocaust and Genocide Studies. Online: http://chgs.umn.edu/histories/armenian/cartoons/ (accessed January 24, 2009).

B.9.c: Poster image from the 1919 film *Ravished Armenia*, The Armenian Genocide Museum-Institute, National Academy of Sciences of the Republic of Armenia Online: www.genocide-museum.am/eng/children/11r.jpg (accessed January 27, 2009).

B.1

The New York Times, April 28, 1915:
"Appeal to Turkey to Stop Massacres"

This article reports a request from the head of the Armenian Church, conveyed by Russian Ambassador Boris Bakhmeteff, to Henry Morgenthau, then American ambassador to Turkey, to ask that Turkish authorities prevent further "religious outbreaks" and "protect imperiled Armenians." The request included an appeal to the American president for aid.

APPEAL TO TURKEY TO STOP MASSACRES

Ambassador Morgenthau Instructed to Make Representations on Request of Russia

WASHINGTON, April 27 — An appeal for relief of Armenian Christians in Turkey, following reported massacres and threatened further outrages, was made to the Turkish Government today by the United States.

Acting upon the request of the Russian Government, submitted through Ambassador Bakhmeteff, Secretary Bryan cabled to Ambassador Morgenthau at Constantinople to make representations to the Turkish authorities asking that steps be taken for the protection of imperiled Armenians and to prevent the recurrence of religious outbreaks.

Ambassador Bakhmeteff called at the State Department late today with a dispatch from his Government, which included an appeal to the President of the United States for aid, forwarded through the Russian Government from the Catholics of the Armenian Church of Etchmiadzin, in the Caucasus.

"The request from the head of the Armenian Church to this Government, forwaded through the Russian Ambassador," said Secretary Bryan, "is the first official notice the department has received of the reported Armenian massacres. Our action was taken as a matter of humanity."

The Russian Embassy today gave out a translation of a recent speech by the Minister of Foreign Affairs in the Duma, in which the presence of Russian troops in Persia was explained. The Foreign Minister said:

"The presence of our troops in Persian territory by no means involves a violation of Persian neutrality. Our detachments were sent to that country some years ago for the definite purpose of establishing and maintaining order in districts contiguous to our possessions, of high economic importance to us, also to prevent the seizure of some of these districts by the Turks, who openly strove to create for themselves there, especially in the district of Urumiah, a convenient base for military operations against the Caucasus. The Persian Government, not having the actual power to maintain its neutrality, met the Turkish violation of the latter with protests, which, however, had no results."

B.2

The Washington Post, April 29, 1915:
"Crucified by Turks"

CRUCIFIED BY TURKS

Christians Are Also Burned Alive, Say Missionaries

SOLDIERS HELP TO MASSACRE

American Missions Invaded and More Than 800 Put to Death

Armenians in Constantinople, to Number of 400, Including Their Patriarch, Thrown Into Jail—United States Citizens Forced to Pay $40,000 Ransom for Refugees—Ambassador Morgenthau Protests to the Porte.

New York, April 28—Details of the massacre of Native Christians at Urumiah, Persia, by Kurds, received today by the Presbyterian Board of Foreign Missions, state that not less that 330 have been murdered there and that not less than 1,000 have perished from disease.

The attacks, it would appear, have not been confined to Kurds, but have been made, in at least one instance, by Turkish soldiers. Crucifixion and burning Christians alive have been revived, missionaries reported to the board.

Turks Attack Americans

The attack in which Turkish soldiers were the assailants, according to reports received by the board, was made upon the American mission and the French Roman Catholic mission. Five native Russian priests, the reports assert, were taken from the American mission by the Turks. It was not known if the priests were hanged.

A report had reached the Presbyterian missionaries at Tabriz that Americans at Urumiah had been forced to pay

$40,000 as a ransom for refugees who had fled to the mission for protection.

These and other matters pertaining to Urumiah were related in two letters received today from Dr. W. S. Vanneman, of Salem, J.N., head of the Presbyterian missions hospital at Tabriz and chairman of the relief committee appointed by the American consul there. Writing from Tabriz, under date of March 14, Dr. Vanneman said:

Tortured, Then Massacred

"About ten days ago the Kurds from Salmas, with the permission of the Turkish troops, gathered all the Nestorian and Armenian men remaining there. It is reported, about 800. Four hundred were sent to Khosrova and 400 to Haft Dewen, under the pretense of giving them bread. They were held a few days and then all of them were tortured and massacred. Many of the women and children were taken away and ill-treated. This happened a day or two before the advancing Russian army took Salmas.

"We are very anxious about Urumiah. A letter dated March 1, from Dr. Shedd (the Rev. Dr. W. A. Shedd, of Marietta, Ohio), came through by messenger two days ago. He said things were getting worse. Culpashan has been plundered and ruined. Fifty-one of the most prominent men of this village were taken out at night, to the cemetery, and shot. The women and girls who could not escape were attacked. This was done by the Turkish Soldiers.

"Forty men had been taken from the Roman Catholic mission by Urumiah city, kept prisoners a few days, then were taken at night two miles from the city and shot."

Under date of March 31, Dr. Vanneman wrote as follows:

"We are more anxious than ever about Urumiah. On the 17th Turkish troops attacked our mission and the Roman Catholic mission and took five native Russian priests from our compound and treated them badly. We do not know yet if they were killed. Mr. Allen was also treated badly because he had sent out three messengers. The gates of the Catholic mission were burned and they were all in great danger. We received word from Ambassador Morgenthau that orders had been sent to Urumiah to protect Christians, but the order was just too late. We are working to get all the remaining Christians away from Urumiah.

Native Christians Crucified

"Some of the native Christian preachers have been crucified and some burned, but these were of other denominations. Dr. Absalomson (a native physician), who had been buried three years, was taken up and his body dishonored. This was done by the owner of villages of which he was overseer. This man has returned and is preaching a holy war.

"I do not believe the real condition of affairs is comprehended in America. It is practically the extermination of the Syrians (Nestorians), and very bad for the Armenians also. The only hope is occupation by Russia."

London, April 28—A Reuter dispatch from Athens says advices from Constantinople are to the effect that Turkish authorities have arrested about 400 Armenians there, including the patriarch, on the pretext that it has been discovered preparations are under way for a rising in the Armenian provinces.

Ambassador Morgenthau, at Constantinople, cabled the State Department yesterday that there was considerable uneasiness in Turkey over the Armenian situation, and that he already had made representations to the Turkish government for the protection of the Armenians.

He referred to one naturalized American who had been threatened.

B.3

The New York Times, October 7, 1915:
"800,000 Armenians Counted Destroyed"

This is a correspondent's report to The New York Times *on proceedings in the British House of Lords, during which James Bryce described the deportations and deaths of Armenians. The report includes a reference to Committee of Union and Progress (CUP) leaders as "the gang now in control of Turkey" and, at the conclusion of the article, a citation of Matthew 27:24, which equates Wilhelm II's alliance with Turkey and "the annihilation by his Turkish ally of a million Christian worshippers of the God he ceaselessly invokes" with Pilate's washing his hands of Jesus' case and relinquishing him to crucifixion.*

800,000 ARMENIANS COUNTED DESTROYED

Viscount Bryce Tells House of Lords That Is the Probable Number of Turks' Victims

10,000 DROWNED AT ONCE

Peers Are Told How Entire Christian Population of Trebizond Was Wiped Out

Special Cable to THE NEW YORK TIMES

LONDON, Oct. 7. — The Daily Chronicle's Parliamentary correspondent in the House of Lords says:

"This afternoon Lord Bryce gave a heart-piercing account of the circumstances under which the Armenian people are being exterminated as a result of an absolutely premeditated policy elaborately pursued by the gang now in control of Turkey. He computes that since May last 800,000 Armenians, men, women, and children, have been slain in cold blood in Asian Minor.

"The House of Lords is a very unemotional assembly, but it was thrilled in every fibre at the story of the horrors compared to which even the atrocities of Abdul Hamid pale. As Lord Bryce truly said, there is not a case in history since the days of Tamerlane where a crime so hideous and on so gigantic a scale has been recorded. An ex-Sultan of Turkey is credited with saying that 'the only way to get rid of the Armenian question is to get rid of the Armenian.'"

"That horrible policy has," Lord Bryce said, "been carried out far more thoroughly by the present Turkish Government than it ever was by Abdul Hamid. The Armenian nation is not yet quite extinct; forlorn remnants have found refuge in the Caucasian provinces; some managed to reach Egypt; a few ill-armed, half-starved bands are bravely defending themselves from would-be assassins in the mountains of Sassun and Cilicia.

"On behalf of these pathetic survivals of a fine race Lord Bryce made a powerful appeal to the neutral nations. He did not mention America by name but it was obvious that this former Ambassador at Washington had the great republic of the West in mind when he appealed to the conscience of neutrals and when he said he believed there are some crimes which even now in the convulsion of a great war the public opinion of the world will not tolerate.

"The Armenian question arose on a question put by Lord Cromer, who asked whether statements that German consular official had been privy to these massacres rest on any substantial evidence. Lord Cromer thinks that though there may be no trustworthy evidence to prove the complicity of the German Government and its agents in these terrible atrocities, yet the German Government, having regard to its influence in Constantinople, cannot be acquitted of moral responsibility unless it can be shown that it took vigorous and energetic measures ot prevent these crimes.

"Lord Crewe, replying for the Government stated that the British Consular reports bear out the story of the massacre and reveal facts of the most horrible character. The condition of refugees in Caucasian provinces is piteous in the extreme.

"'We have no official confirmation,' said Lord Crewe, 'of the allegations that German Consular representatives have not merely looked on but have possibly managed these horrors. Statements to that effect have, however, been freely made by American observers, and in view of what has happened, elsewhere, these cannot be said to be antecedently improbable since July last, when we informed the Porte that individuals who incited these massacres would be held personally responsible by us, no representations on this subject have been made by our Foreign office to the Turkish Government either directly or indirectly, but they know our views.'"

The Daily News commenting on the Armenian massacres says:

"How much does Wilhelm II. know? What views has the Proctor of Islam on the annihilation by his Turkish ally of a million Christian worshippers of the God he ceaselessly invokes? Does he indorse Count Reventlow's dispassionate judgment that 'it is not only right, but even a duty to take vigorous measures against the unreliable, bloodthirsty, riotous Armenian elements if the Turkish authorities think it right to do so?' For a German, he adds, there can, of course, be no meddling.

"For a German, of course, there cannot. America's horror struck appeal to Turkey's ally will be laughed to scorn. 'And Pilate took water and washed his hands before the multitude, saying, "I am innocent of the blood of this just person."'"

B.4

The New York Times, November 1, 1915:
"Aid for Armenians Blocked by Turkey"

This is a detailed account of the horrors of deportation and exile, issued by the American Committee on Armenian Atrocities (note members Cleveland Dodge and Charles Crane). In the article, Turkish officials frame their actions as "a military measure to protect them against a possible attack of a race that is disloyal." The committee reports cabling $106,000 to Morgenthau in Constantinople for relief efforts.

AID FOR ARMENIANS BLOCKED BY TURKEY

Attempts to Send Food to Refugees Frustrated, Says the American Committee.

PUTS VICTIMS AT 1,000,000

Careful Survey Shows 55,000 Persons Killed in the Vilayet of Van Alone.

The American Committee on Armenian Atrocities, among the members of which are Cardinal Gibbons, Cleveland H. Dodge, Bishop David H. Greer, Oscar S. Straus, Professor Samuel T. Dutton, Charles R. Crane, and many other prominent citizens, issued a statement yesterday in which it was said that authentic reports from Turkey proved that the war of extermination being waged by the Turks against the Armenians was so terrible that when all the facts were known the world would realize that what had been done was "the greatest, most pathetic, and most arbitrary tragedy in history.

Attempts to furnish food to the Armenians ordered deported to distant parts of the empire were blocked by the Turkish authorities, the committee said, the Turkish officials stating that "they wished nothing to be done that would prolong their lives."

In the statement the committee makes public a report received a few days ago from an official representative of one of the neutral powers, who, reporting on conditions in one of the Armenian camps, says:

"I have visited their encampment and a more pitiable sight cannot be imagined. They are, almost without exception, ragged, hungry and sick. This is not surprising in view of the fact that they have been on the road for nearly two months, with no change of clothing, no chance to bathe, no shelter and little to eat. I watched them one time when their food was brought. Wild animals could not be worse. They rushed upon the guards who carried the food and the guards beat them back with clubs, hitting hard enough to kill sometimes. To watch them one could hardly believe these people to be human beings. As one walks through the camp, mothers offer their children and beg you to take them. In fact, the Turks have been taking their choice of these children and girls for slaves or worse. There are very few men among them, as most of the men were killed on the road. Women and children were also killed. The entire movement seems to be the most thoroughly organized and effective massacre this country has ever seen."

"They all agree," adds the committee, referring to the reports, "as to the method of procedure, the thoroughness and cruelty of the destructive work, and the confessed purpose of the plan to wipe out the Armenian nation. The fact that the central government at Constantinople refuses to permit Armenians to leave the country is further evidence of their purpose of extermination.

"The Turks do not deny the atrocities, but claim they are a military measure to protect them against a possible attack of a race that is disloyal.

"It is impossible to estimate how many have already perished. A careful survey in the Van Vilayet gathered the names of 55,000 persons who had been killed. Others were able to escape by flight to Persia and Russia. An eyewitness who has recently made an extended journey across Asian Minor saw over 50,000 poor, dazed, helpless, starving refugees camped by the roadside in a region almost desert, with no provision for their food supply. Probably it is not an overestimate to say that 1,000,000 of the possible 2,000,000 Armenians in Turkey at the beginning of the war are either dead or in Moslem harems, or forced to profess Mohammedanism, or are on their sad journey to the desert and death."

The committee says it has cabled $106,000 to Ambassador Morgenthau at Constantinople, of which $100,000 was for relief of Armenians in Turkey, and the remainder for Armenians who had escaped into Egypt. The office of the committee, of which Mr. Crane is Treasurer, is at 70 Fifth Avenue.

B.5

The New York Times, December 15, 1915:
"Million Armenians Killed or in Exile"

A statement from the American Committee for Armenian and Syrian Relief (which was to become the Near East Relief that sent Mary to Hadjin) outlining "further atrocities committed by Turks upon Armenian Christians." A large portion of the statement is based upon a letter from "a missionary station in Konia."

MILLION ARMENIANS KILLED OR IN EXILE

American Committee on Relief Says Victims of Turks Are Steadily Increasing.

POLICY OF EXTERMINATION

More Atrocities Detailed in Support of Charge That Turkey Is Acting Deliberately.

In a statement issued yesterday from the offices of the American Committee for Armenian an dSyrian Relief at 70 Fifth Avenue further atrocities committed by Turks upon Armenian Christians were detailed and additional evidence was given to support Lord Bryce's assertion that the massacres are the result of a deliberate plan of the Turkish Government to "get rid of the Armenian question," as Abdul Hamid once said, by getting "rid of the Armenians."

Professor Samuel T. Dutton, Secretary of the committee, said:

"According to all of the best evidence which the American committee has received, it is probably well within the truth to say that of the 2,000,000 Armenians in Turkey a year ago, at least 1,000,000 have been killed or forced into Islam, or compelled to flee the country, or have died upon the way to exile, or are now upon the road to the deserts of Northern Arabia, or are already there. The number of victims is constantly increasing. Surely there can be no greater need of immediate help, even in these troublous times, than the desperate need of the Armenian refugees. The American committee has already done much in collecting and sending funds, as has also the English committee, but there is still the direst need of generous contributions. All contributions should be sent to Charles R. Crane, Treasurer, 70 Fifth Avenue."

Walter H. Mallory, Executive Secretary of American Committee, said that the committee was in close touch with the Lord Mayor's committee of London and that "daily authentic reports of almost unbelievable atrocities" were received. In the statement made public, there was an excerpt from a letter received by the American committee from the English committee, which read:

"The committee knows that there are 180,000 refugees still in the Caucasus besides 30,000 who have died there, and 70,000 who have returned to parts of Turkey and Persia."

A large part of the statement is taken up with a letter received by the American committee form a missionary stationed in Konia. In part, the letter read:

"Soon after the great deportation that preceded the arrival of the new Vali Miss C. and I drove out to Kachin Han, the first station of the railroad towards Eregli, just to follow the crowd,

as a large number had been driven off on foot with the expectation of taking the railroad later on. Kachin Han is about three hours from here by carriage, and even so near to Konia as this we found about one hundred people, waiting and lying about the station in utter desolation. They had been there three days; most of them had eaten up all the provisions they had and looked haggard and emaciated, veritable famine victims such as one sees in pictures of a scene in India.

"The train from Konia arrived while we were there, and the greater number of the people dragged themselves to the cars in an effort to get on board, but were pushed back by the gendarmes, partly because they had no tickets and partly because there was no room; so the poor people were forced to turn back to where they had been sitting or lying about the station.

"Among the hundred people there were not half a dozen tents, and the half dozen were improvised and of the flimsiest character. Most of the people were lying out in the open day and night, many of them without even blankets or quilts. Half a mile from the station I found two old women who were crawling off on hands and knees, too weak to walk; they had been carried off on a wagon ostensibly to go to a village, but once out of sight of the gendarmes, the driver had dropped them in the field and hurried away. Without exception, all of the people looked forward to certain death by starvation, nor was there any other future to be seen for them."

B.6

The Christian Herald, November 1, 1916:
"God Save Armenia!"

This article from The Christian Herald *offers a good example of the Christian rhetoric that informed calls for financial contributions from "churches, Christian Endeavor Societies, Baptist Young People's Societies, Sunday schools, and all similar organizations," while reporting on the deportations: "These people represent the oldest existing form of Christianity, and it was in the effort to exterminate them for this reason, and because they would not accept an alien religion, that they have suffered so much. There is probably no country known in recorded history whose people have suffered so heavily for the Christian faith as Armenia."*

GOD SAVE ARMENIA!

There are many indications of a great national response to the appeal in behalf of suffering Armenia and Syria. When President Wilson issued his recent proclamation setting apart Saturday, October 21, and Sunday, October 22, as days upon which the American people might make their contributions for the aid of those stricken races, he gave the weight and dignity of high official emphasis and approbation to a work which had already begun, but which needed vigorous reinforcement.

It is shown by consular reports that these remote districts have been scenes of slaughter and suffering on a scale that is appalling. Before the war, the Armenian population of Turkey, Persia and Syria was estimated at two million souls. Of these, 750,000 have been massacred or died of wounds, disease or exhaustion. Of the 1,200,000 survivors, a million are destitute and starving. These include not only Armenians but Nestorians and other native Christians in Turkey, Persia, Syria and Palestine—all Bible lands. These people represent the oldest existing form of Christianity, and it was the effort to exterminate them for this reason, and because they would not accept an alien religion, that they have suffered so much. There is probably no country known in recorded history whose people have suffered so heavily for the Christian faith as Armenia."

There are today 500,000 homeless and destitute refugees in Damascus, Zor and Aleppo dependent on charity. In Turkey proper there are 300,000 more in the same pitiful condition, and 200,000 in Persia, Anatolia and the Caucasus.

The Armenian Committee for Armenian and Syrian Relief made the following announcement on October 11:

CHRISTIAN HERALD LEADS WITH $15,000 FOR ARMENIAN RELIEF IN RESPONSE TO PRESIDENT'S APPEAL.

The first large gift—$15,000—in response to President Wilson's appeal for the suffering Armenians and Syrians reached the office of Charles R. Crane, treasurer of the American Committee for Armenian and Syrian Relief, 70 Fifth Avenue, this morning. It was from the Emergency Relief Fund of the Christian Herald. The check received this morning makes a total of $20,000 which the Christian Herald has sent to Armenia: $5,000 having been cabled some time ago through the State Department to representatives of the Committee in Turkey.

The editors and management of the Herald are entering into a wider publicity campaign in behalf of these suffering peoles and stated today that the check just received would be followed by others as rapidly as possible until provision had been made for at least the necessities of life for these people.

Among the letters received by the Armenian and Syrian Relief Committee in New York is one from Dor el Zor, Syria, which tells how the little children are dying of hunger. It tells of young girls being sold for bread by half-crazed parents, and of mothers throwing themselves into the rivers, rather than see their starving children die. A letter from Hamam tells of a camp of a thousand Armenians in tents, and all the occupants perishing slowly of hunger and misery, gnawing bones and eating grain refuse and grass. A letter from Sepka, another concentration point, tells of 2,500 refugees, gaunt as skeletons, with many deaths daily and grave-diggers always busy. At Etchmiadzin 11,000 died of starvation, and 40,000 more in the surrounding country. Refugees arriving there were almost naked. Six thousand of these unfortunates were deported to Ana, five hundred being killed on the way by Arabs. At a place called Haleb there are 25,000 little orphans whose parents have perished in the cruel persecution. In a village of 450 souls the solitary survivor was one woman who escaped the general slaughter almost by a miracle.

The Christian Herald has no desire to shock the hearts of its readers by a recital of these horrors; but the truth, the great outstanding facts of the situation, must be told. Our American missionaries, in conjunction with our consular representatives, are doing all that lies within their power to help the destitute survivors. It is a fortunate thing that they are able to accomplish even this. They are looking to us to supply the means of saving life and alleviating suffering.

CHRISTIAN AMERICA has done much for Armenia in the past, and now, in the hour of that country's direst need, we cannot turn a deaf ear to the despairing cry of the perishing ones. American has done noble work in helping Belgium, Poland and Serbia, and in many other ways in softening the blows inflicted by the war, which have fallen on the helpless women and children and the non-combatants. We must now make an effort to save Armenia, to gather up the remnant of this ancient Christian people and feed, shelter and clothe them, under our protection in their own land.

Every reader of the Christian Herald can help in this great life-saving campaign conducted "In His Name." You can do this by sending your contribu-

tion *today* to the Christian Herald, which is working hand in hand with the Relief Committee and the missionaries. Remember that every dollar given to this worthy cause goes undiminished, in the care of the State Department at Washington, and that the donor has therefore the highest assurance that his gift will reach the mark. Churches, Epworth Leagues, Christian Endeavor Societies, Baptist Young People's Societies, Sunday schools, and all similar organizations will find here a glorious opportunity for the most practical kind of Christian benevolence.

We have shown you the need; now do your share, and send with your gift a prayer that God may make it a means of saving one life, of rescuing one poor sufferer from starvation; of bringing a ray of comfort into one sad family group in these scattered homes. Let our prayer be "God save Armenia," and let us try to help him to do it.

B.7

The New York Times, July 27, 1919:
"Armenian Tells of Death Pilgrimage"

In a letter to his sister, excerpted in this article, an unidentified Armenian shared the story of his deportation. His sister sent the letter to The New York Times *to be published. The story is very much like the story of Menas Effendi retold in Blanche Eby's memoirs. (See Appendix E.2 for the relevant excerpt.)*

ARMENIAN TELLS OF DEATH PILGRIMAGE

Writes to Sister in New York of Cruelties Suffered from the Turks.

FAMILY IS TORN FROM HIM

Children Taken Away and Wife Sold Into Slavery in Journey Across Desert.

A tale of cruelty by the Turks to Armenians is told in a letter just received by a New York woman from her brother, who, with his family, was part of the great host that was driven from their homes. The refugee had his two children torn from him, and he saw his wife sold into slavery. He saw his countrymen beaten or stabbed to death, and hundreds left to die from hunger and sickness as they were being driven from place to place.

The letter ws sent to THE TIMES by the sister, who has received word that her brother is back in his native town after five years of suffering and wandering.

"It was on a Tuesday morning in August, 1914," the letter says, "when our priest was called by the Turkish Government and was told that all Armenians of Ofion-Kara-Hisean should get ready within forty-eight hours to be deported.

"Long before the time given in which we were to make our preparations the Turkish gendarmes came. With whips, and by beating, they compelled us to leave everything and go to the railroad station. Here they gave us tickets to Konia only.

"We reached Konia in the night. A few days later Brother Hagop, with his family, were sent here. Upon seeing each other we resolved not to part until the end. But here, too, the head police soon began to put into practice the cruel and vicious plans of Valy Pasha of the said Province, and ordered the refugees, numbering about 5,000 to 6,000 families, deported.

Families Torn Apart.

"Those who were in their homes were made to come out; others who were caught in the market place were killed or imprisoned. Women were separated from their husbands, children from their mothers. We, too, were thus broken up, and I lost trace of the children and my wife; also of my brother and his family.

"We were set on the road again. This time the caravan was headed for Tarsus. Fortunately, the children and my wife happened to be in the same caravan that I was in, and we once more were together. While we were marching the Turkish soldiers, with drawn swords, suddenly made their way through the crowd, and, like beasts let loose in a flock of sheep, killed and wounded many. The rest still dragged on under the influence of the bloody swords until Ras-ul-Ain Desert was reached. This place was especially noted for the carrying on of their butchery, for all that were sent to these parts were sent there to die."

B.8

The Independent, February 28, 1920:
"Shall Armenia Perish?"

This article is Henry Morgenthau's call, a year after the armistice, for continued aid to Armenian survivors. The article leads with the declaration that "two hundred and fifty thousand Christian Armenian women enslaved in Turkish harems call to the people of America for liberation."

Shall Armenia Perish?
By Henry Morgenthau

Former Ambassador to Turkey and National Vice-Chairman of Near East Relief

Two hundred and fifty thousand Christian Armenian women enslaved in Turkish harems call to the people of America for liberation! One hundred thousand women already rescued by Near East Relief agents from harems will perish unless support from America is continued! Two hundred and fifty thousand children, orphaned by the unspeakable Turks, are calling in the only English they know, "Bread, Uncle Sam." One million two hundred thousand destitute, homeless, clotheless adults look to the giant in the West for the succor that will keep them from annihilation. What shall our answer be?

If they were good enough to fight and die for us when we needed their help so sorely, are they not good enough to be given some crumbs from our plenty?

Since the beginning of the war, the Turkish Armenians have been largely refugees. A simple, agricultural people, they have been exiled from their farms and deprived of all opportunity to support themselves. Now, more than a year after the armistice, they are still living the life of nomads, able to continue alive only by virtue of American philanthropy. If ever unmerited suffering called for succor the plight of the Armenians should be heeded now. A few months more and it may be relief will come too late for those myriads whom only we can save.

Let the American slogan now become—Serve Armenians for a little while longer with life's necessities that they may be preserved for the day of national freedom and rebirth, which no people more truly and greatly deserves.

The belief, held by some persons, that Turkey has repented and can do no further harm, is without foundation. The group that led Turkey into the war on the side of Germany is now in the saddle. The Turk has not been disarmed and these leaders are now aiding the Tartars. Kurds and Bolshevists are urging them on to kill and rob the surviving Armenians at every opportunity. The deportations and massacres during the war were not spontaneous uprisings of unorganized mobs, but were the working out of a well-plotted plan of wholesale extermination in which regular Turkish officers and troops took part as if in a campaign against an enemy in the field.

More than 2,000,000 persons were deported. They system was about the same everywhere. The Armenians, men, women, and children, would be assembled in the marketplace. Then the able-bodied men would be marched off and killed by being shot or clubbed in cold blood at some spot which did not necessitate the trouble of burial.

Next the women would be sorted out. Agents of the Turk officers picked the youngest and fairest for their masters' harems. Next the civil officials had their pick, and then the remainder either were sold for one medjidi—a silver coin valued at about 80 cents—or were driven forth to be seized by the lower class Turks and Kurds.

As a last step, those who remained, mothers, grandmothers, children, were driven forth on their death pilgrimages across the desert of Aleppo, with no food, no water, no shelter, to be robbed and beaten at every halt, to see children slain in scores before their eyes, and babies dashed to death against rocks or spitted on the bayonets of the soldier guards.

If American is going to condone these offenses, if she is going to permit to continue conditions that threaten and permit their repetition, she is party to the crime. These peoles must be freed from the agony and danger of such horrors. They must not only be saved for the present but either thru governmental action or protection under the League of Nations they must be given assurance that they will be free in peace and that no harm can come to them.

New York

B.9

Popular Media Images

B.9.a

American and British Relief Posters about Armenia, c. 1915

In this section are featured a selection of fundraising posters published and distributed by the American Committee for Relief in the Near East and Near East Relief, most intensively in 1918. They sometimes represent America as a female figure of Justice. Many depict Armenia as a child or mother-and-child.

B.9.b

Editorial Cartoons of the Armenian Genocide

This selection of editorial cartoons comment on conditions in Armenia and international response, or lack thereof. They appeared in the Western press—some, during the earlier period of Hamidian massacres in 1894-1897 and 1910, and others, right before or during the period of the memoirs, encompassing the deportations and their aftermath immediately following World War I.

ENFER PASHA

N.B. Instead of calling the Turkish minister responsible of the massacres of 1915 by his name ENVER, the newspaper calls him ENFER which in French means HELL.

—*La Baïonnette* (Paris)

EUROPA (to the new Sultan)— *"As you're a young Turk, Sir, I count on you to make a clean sweep of the old methods."*

—*Punch* (London)

NIX ON ENTANGLING ALLIANCE NO.1

—(THOMAS) *Detroit News*, April, 1919

GO AWAY!

—(KIRBY) *New York World,* 1920

"IT AIN'T POLITE TO INTERRUPT!"

—(SYKES) *Evening Public Ledger* (Philadelphia), June, 1922

THERE WAS A TIME WHEN THE WHOLE
HUMAN RACE WAS INTERESTED IN
ARMENIA

BUT NOW THE HUMAN RACE IS INTERESTED
ELSEWHERE

—(MC CUTCHEON) *Chicago Tribune*, June, 1920

Dayton News.]   [U.S.A.
"Bah, the price of Massacre is Oil!"

Dayton, Ohio, daily newspaper, 1924,
after the signing of the Treaty of Lausanne

B.9.c

Ravished Armenia

This promotional poster was for the 1919 Hollywood film Ravished Armenia, *which was based on the memoirs of Arshaluys (Aurora) Mardiganian.*

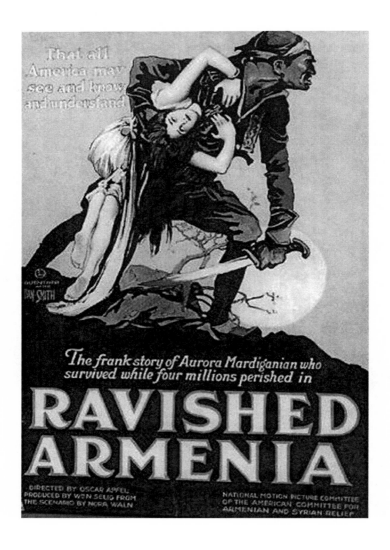

APPENDIX C

Armenian Resistance: Nationalist, Independence, and Revolutionary Movements

C.1: *The Manitoba Free Press*, "Armenians Besiege Van," November 7, 1914.

C.2: *The New York Times*, "Turkish Armenians in Armed Revolt," November 13, 1914.

C.3: *The Times* (London), "The Armenian Red Cross to the Editor of the *Times*," January 12, 1915.

C.4: *The New York Times*, "Accuse Armenians of Wronging Turks," October 22, 1915.

C.5: Armenian Revolutionary Federation Documents

    C.5.a: "Federation of Armenian Revolutionaries Manifesto," Summer 1890, Armenian Revolutionary Federation, Western U.S.A. website,http://www.arf1890.com/PDF/Dzerakir%20program/A RF%0MANIFESTO%20-%20English.pdf.

    C.5.b: "May 30, 1918 Declaration of Independence of the Armenian National Council," Armenian Revolutionary Federation Archives Institute, http://arfarchives.org/.

    C.5.c: "Fedayees under the banner of the Armenian Revolutionary Federation (c. 1890-1896)," http://en.wikipedia.org/wiki/ File: Fedayees.JPG.

C.1

The Manitoba Free Press, November 7, 1914:
"Armenians Beseige Van"

This is a brief dispatch from London reporting that Armenians, "aiding the Russians," were laying siege to the city of Van, presumably looking to arm themselves from the town's large arsenal.

Armenians Besiege Van

London, Nov. 7.—A dispatch received by the Daily Telegraph from Tiflis, capital of the Lieutenancy of Caucasia, by way of Moscow, says:

"The Turkish town of Van (140 miles southeast of Erzerum, Turkish Armenia) is being besieged by a detachment of Armenians who are aiding the Russians. The Town has a large arsenal. Another Armenian detachment is operating in the rear of the Turkish army.

C.2

The New York Times, November 13, 1914:
"Turkish Armenians in Armed Revolt"

This article presents reports from Petrograd that "Armenian students" and "Armenian peasants" were ready and preparing to collaborate with the Russian army in the war against Turkey. Quoting an Armenian newspaper, the Times *reported that thousands of guerilla bands were causing heavy losses to the Turks.*

TURKISH ARMENIANS IN ARMED REVOLT

Were Ready to Join Russian Invaders, Having Drilled and Collected Arms.

SEE DAY OF DELIVERANCE

Native Paper Says They Are Prepared for Any Sacrifice— Refuse to Join Turkish Army.

PETROGRAD, Nov. 12. — Reports reaching the Russian capital from the Turkish border attach increasing importance to the part the Armenians are playing in the Russo-Turkish war.

In several towns occupied by the Russians the Armenian students have shown themselves ready to join the invading army, explaining that they had prepared themselves for the Russian approach by constant drilling and by gathering arms secretly. All along the line of march, according to these dispatches, the Armenian peasants are receiving the Russian troops with enthusiasm and giving provisions to them freely.

An Armenian newspaper, referring to this crisis in the history of Armenia, publishes the following:

"The long-anticipated day of deliverance for the Turkish Armenians is at hand, and the Armenians are prepared for any sacrifice made necessary by the performance of their manifest duty."

From this border country there have come to Petrograd further reports of armed conflicts arising from the refusal of Armenians to become Turkish conscripts and to surrender their arms.

It is now rumored that the important City of Van is today besieged by Armenian guerrilla bands in great force. In Feitun the number of insurgents is said to exceed 20,000, and they are reported to have defeated all the Turkish troops sent against them, causing heavy losses to the Turks.

C.3

The Times (London), January 12, 1915:
"The Armenian Red Cross to the Editor of the *Times*"

This letter to the Editor of the Times *is a plea from the Armenian Red Cross to the British public for financial and clothing contributions to support volunteer Armenian and Armenian-American soldiers "fighting for the Russians in Turkey."*

THE ARMENIAN RED CROSS TO THE EDITOR OF THE TIMES.

Sir.—We are asking the public to support the above work, which is in need of immediate assistance. There are now in the field more than 8,000 Armenian volunteers fighting for the Russians in Turkey; 5,000 more are in the United States ready to sail. They have been equipped and are maintained by Armenians all over the world at a cost of £6,000 per day. By the spring it is expected that there will be between 20,000 and 25,000 altogether in the field. At present they have no doctor, and there are only five untrained Armenian ladies assisting as nurses. Fifteen medical students from Kieff are now on their way to the front to assist, but there are no Red Cross appliances of any sort, and these are urgently needed. There has been heavy fighting around Bashkale, which the volunteers have captured, supported by columns of Russian Regulars mainly composed of Armenians. The snow is 3 ft. deep, and there have been many very serious cases of frostbite. There are now 12,000 Armenian refugees at Sarikamysch alone to be provided for. These are being cared for as far as possible for the moment by the Russian Armenian inhabitants, who are themselves very poor owing to floods having spoilt their last crops. Hundreds of old men, women, and children have tramped through the snow without shoes or stockings, these articles having been seized by Turkish soldiers, who had been billeted in their houses.

In many instances these wretched people were driven out just as they were by the Turkish soldiers as they entered the villages, The Catholicos (head of the Armenian church) and his clergy, with local committees, are rendering all the assistance possible, but they have no funds left, all the money subscribed by Armenians having to go to the upkeep of the volunteers.

The Armenian Society, composed of British and American people, is administering the Red Cross and Refugee Fund free of all cost, while the British Consul-General at Moscow is cooperating. The Russian authorities are separating the fugitives as much as possible, as it is feared there may be an outbreak of disease, owing to their famished and impoverished condition. It is to the generous heart of the great British public that we make this appeal. Donations of money may be sent to the hon. treasurer, Mr. H. A. Godson Bohn, at 17, Holland Villas-road, Kensington. Gifts of warm woolen clothing, including mufflers, gloves, cardigans, stockings, socks, and bandages for the volunteers, and warm garments of any kind and boots in good condition for the refugees will be gratefully received and acknowledged by the hon. secretary. ISABEL SOMERSET,

LUCY C. F. CAVENDISH
(President, "Friends of Armenia"),
BRYCE.

C.4

The New York Times, October 22, 1915:
"Accuse Armenians of Wronging Turks"

This article foregrounds the ways in which the press was used, by both Armenian sympathizers and the Turks, as political advocacy. It reports "countercharges" filed with the Times *by the Turkish government, "that barbarous acts have been committed on Moslems along the Caucasian frontier by Russian troops, aided by members of the Greek and Armenian populations of that region." The report from General Ottoman Headquarters included graphic accounts of attacks on women and children. Note the lack of comment or response on the part of the American State Department.*

ACCUSE ARMENIANS OF WRONGING TURKS

Ottoman Authorities Give Out Formal Charges of Widespread Outrages

ALONG CAUCASIAN FRONTIER

Russian Troops Linked with Greek and Armenian Civilians as the Perpetrators

Special to the New York Times.

WASHINGTON, Oct. 21.—Following world-wide accusations of barbarous treatment of the Christians of Armenia, the Turkish Government has filed counter-charges here, in which it is alleged that barbarous acts have been committed on Moslems along the Caucasian frontier by Russian troops, aided by members of the Greek and Armenian population of that region.

The countercharge was sent by the Turkish Government to its Embassy at Washington. It took the form of a communications which was delivered to Secretary Lansing today by Abdul Hak Hussein Bey, First Secretary and Chargé d'Affaires of the Embassy since Oct. 4, 1914, when he took charge upon the return of Ambassador A. Rustem Bey to Turkey.

After delivering the communication to Secretary Lansing the Turkish Chargé handed a summary of it to the press.

Secretary Lansing refrained from commenting upon the Turkish Government's communication, beyond saying that he had not had the opportunity to examine the document. It is not expected that the State Department will take any action on the communication at this time, but will file it for future reference.

The summary given out by Hussem Bey says:

"The Ottoman Embassy has just received an official report from the General Ottoman headquarters concerning the barbarous acts perpetrated by the Russian troops, assisted by the Greek and Armenian populations, against the Moslems dwelling along the frontier of the Caucasus. These atrocious acts, committed under the eyes of the Russian authorities in the districts of Tavashguerd, Pensguerd, Olti, and Ardanuche have been well ascertained after a careful inquiry by Seifullah Effendi, a member of the Ottoman Parliament from Erzorum. Some of the most typical cases are related below,

with omission however of certain details which could not be printed on account of their indescribable horror.

"A band of Russians and Armenians repaired to the house of Murad Bey, a wealthy man of the village of Kirechud, well-known for his charitable acts toward all the inhabitants, without distinction of race or creed, with the obvious intention of assaulting his old wife. Murad Bey realized the impossibility of rescuing her from dishonor, killed her with his own gun, and was himself later murdered by the aggressors. The fury of the latter was then directed against the daughter-in-law of Murad Bey, whose son, Sulleyman, following the example of his father, was also murdered.

"The offenders went afterward to the village of Izensur, and in order to prevent the repetition of similar acts, began by shutting up in a barn the male part of the population and after that assaulted the women. The Moslems of the surrounding villages, being forewarned of the danger, rushed to the spot, but too late to rescue the women, among whom two girls 13 years of age died from disgrace and torture.

"Moslem women who took refuge in the village of Parishur were assaulted by Greeks and Armenians, and some of them had to submit to the worst treatment. Most of them, however, preferring death to disgrace, threw themselves from a hill 200 meters high into a rocky precipice, where they all perished.

"A great number of Moslem women at Ardanuche who had fled to Tavasguerd had to endure the same fate.

"Whilst they had been left half dead, their Russian, Armenian, and Greek aggressors carried the cruelty to the point of piercing with their bayonets the cheeks of their babies in order to prevent them from taking the milk of their mothers. In this wise, mothers and children perished by a slow and terrible death under the yes of their persecutors.

"The wife and the daughter of Ibrahim Allaa Ibo were carried away by Greeks and Armenians from the village of Mokdjaiar to the village of Pertek in the district of Olti, and there they were assaulted. Two Mussulmans, rushing to their aid, rescued the young girl. The mother died after having received twenty-one wounds. The young girl lost her life two months later as a consequence of the shock she had experienced.

"Armenians and Greeks serving as guides to the troops, in the attack on the village of Erghenes, have assaulted with unheard of brutality the wife of Imam Oglou Osman Agha, under the eyes of her helpless husband. The latter was afterward murdered and his body cut to pieces.

"Zabra, wife of Mouhib Oglou Mohammed Ali, equally from the village of Erghenes, 18 years old, was tortured by the same malefactors during three days, after which she was killed and her body horribly mutilated.

"The Armenians dwelling in the village of Dauzote beheaded a certain man, Cherif by name, and four other Mussulmans, who had taken refuge in that village.

"A Greek, named Yani, murdered in the middle of the street and before a numerous assemblage, Garib Agha of the village of Karnavas, in the district of Tavasguerd, who had fled to the village of Azort, in the district of Tortum. The Armenians who were witnessing this scene joined Yani at once and dragged twenty-five Mussulmans out from the houses where they had concealed themselves. Driven into the street, these unfortunate people were called together and all of them killed, after having experience horrible tortures recalling the Middle Ages. Their bodies, cut to pieces, were then exhibited on every street corner.

"The same murderers proceeded to the village of Djihan, and there they attacked five aged men, 70 years old. These were first covered with wounds, and afterward, being smeared over the kerosene, were burned alive.

"These few instances could be multiplied, but they are sufficient to show the barbarous spirit with which the Russians, aided by Armenians and Greeks, are carrying on the war in the Caucasus."

C.5

Armenian Revolutionary
Federation Documents

During the late 19th and early 20th centuries, several nationalist groups—including the Armenian Patriotic Society (1885), the Armenian Social Democratic (Hunchak) party (1887), and the Armenian Revolutionary Federation (ARF)-Dashnak party (1890)—surfaced in response to Ottoman repressions. Of these, the ARF-Dashnak party may be the most salient to Mary's narrative, since the ARF organized itself into small armed resistance groups (fedayees) and, among other things, attempted to defend Armenian towns and villages. They were active in the Armenian-Tatar massacres of 1905-1907 and led the Armenian National Council that declared the independence of the Armenian state in March 1918. The following political documents and photographs provide some sense of the movement, its aspirations, and its actions.

C.5.a

"Federation of Armenian Revolutionaries Manifesto," Summer 1890, at Tiflis

This statement of nationalist solidarity was a precarious mediation of the socialist ideals of the newly joining pro-Marxist Hunchakian Revolutionary Party and the liberation focus of the non-socialist nationalist revolutionaries in the Federation. It is the only extant document from the first meeting of the Federation in Tiflis in the summer of 1890. It is arresting in its impatience with dependence on European alliances: "The race now understands that its power lies within itself. Yesterday's helpless and patient Armenian is today a revolutionary."

MANIFESTO

Fellow Armenians,

Today the Armenian cause is entering a new era. For centuries, Western Armenian has been enserfed and demanding freedom.

It was only yesterday that the Armenian begged with his head bowed for assistance from the western world. Today he is convinced that placing his hope on others is in vain, and he has vowed to protect his rights, his being, his honor and his family with his very own hands.

The Armenian people have for centuries lived under Turkish oppression. They have planted and attended for centuries, only to see the fruits of their labor ravished by their tyrant rulers. Through the centuries they have ruined Armenian sanctities, but the Armenian people have bared it all, bared it with patience, and have continued to flood their soil with their sweat. . . . It was as if the Armenian people were willing to show the world that it is possible to bring about freedom through civilized means. Modern Europe promised to put an end to Turkish plunders in Armenia. However, year passed after year, and the situation of Armenians in Armenia not only did not improve, but also intensified and has since become so hellish and unbearable, that even this remarkably patient race is unable to continue its existence.

Patience has its limits however. The intolerable abuses finally awakened Armenians; today, they have vowed either to die or to be free. And as Erzrum and Constantinople stand boldly in complaint, Armenians no longer beg, but demand and demand with arms in hand. . . . Today Europe sees in front of it a complete people, a complete race, which has begun to protect its human rights.

The race now understands that its power lies within itself. Yesterday's help-less and patient Armenian is today a revolutionary.

The forbearer of this revolutionary ideology is the Armenian Revolutionary Federation, who hereby invites all Armenians to unite under a common flag. Although the Armenian Revolutionary Federation is newly becoming an orga-nizational entity, its roots are old and experience through the organizations, which merged in its creation. The Armenian Revolutionary Federation is going to work on uniting all forces, bringing together their centers. By setting as its goal the political and economic freedom of Western Armenia, the Armenian Revolutionary Federation has involved itself in the struggle initiated by the people themselves against the Turkish regime, vowing to fight until the very last drop of blood in the name of freedom. Let us all unite with the people, who have raised the flag of freedom. He who does not follow and turns away from the people is an enemy of the people. And in particular, you, the youth, defend-ers of ideology always and everywhere, may you unite with your people.

And you, the elderly, may you support and inspire the youth with your wis-dom and experience.

And you, the wealthy, may you open up your riches and support those who confront the enemy with an open chest.

And you, the Armenian woman, may you breed inspiration into this holy cause.

And you, the clergy, may you bless the soldier who fights for freedom.

There is no time to wait.

Let us unite, O Armenians, and let us bravely advance the holy cause of achieving freedom.

FEDERATION OF ARMENIAN REVOLUTIONARIES

C.5.b

May 30, 1918, Declaration of Independence
of the Armenian National Council

In the midst of the splintering of its alliances within the Transcaucasian Federative Republic, and declarations of independence by Georgia and Azerbaijan, the Armenian National Council sent representatives to Batum to negotiate peace on behalf of the Armenian people and crafted the vague statement below, one which does not even claim out-right independence or official status as a republic for the Armenian provinces. See Richard G. Hovannisian, The Armenian Republic: The First Year, 1918-1919, *for a detailed analysis of these developments.*

"In view of the complete political collapse of the Trans-Caucasus and the new situation created by the proclamation of the independence of Georgia and Azerbaijan, the Armenian National Council declares itself the supreme and sole administration of the Armenian provinces. Due to certain grave circumstances that prevent us from forming an Armenian National Government, the Armenian National Council temporarily assumes all governmental functions in order to pilot the political and administrative leadership of the Armenia provinces."

C.5.c

"Fedayees under the banner of the Armenian Revolutionary Federation, c.1890-1896"

The banner reads: "*Azadoutioun gam mah*"
("Liberty or Death")

APPENDIX D

Press Coverage of the 1919–1920 Siege of Hadjin

D.1: *The New York Times*, "Besieged Four Weeks, Hadjin Calls for Aid," April 16, 1920.

D.2: *The New York Times,* "Turks Take Hadjin," November 2, 1920.

D.3: *The New York Times,* "Armenians Complain of French," by Arshag Mahdesian, November 5, 1920.

D.1

The New York Times, April 16, 1920:
"Besieged Four Weeks, Hadjin Calls for Aid"

This article reports on the ongoing siege of Hadjin, including an Armenian plea for French military aid, just two months before the Near East Relief compound fell to the Nationalists and Mary and the other relief workers fled over the mountains to Constantinople. The city held out until the following November. (See Appendix D.2.)

BESIEGED FOUR WEEKS, HADJIN CALLS FOR AID

6,000 Armenians There, in Peril of Massacre by Turks, Appeal to French.

Special to the New York Times.

WASHINGTON, April 15.—Information received today by the Armenian National Union of America indicates that the situation in Cilicia continues precarious. Fighting is reported in progress between the forces of Mustapha Kemal Pasha, the Turkish Nationalist leader, and the surviving Armenians.

The siege of Hadjin, which lasted four weeks, has not been raised. The Armenians there, it is stated, are holding their positions against overwhelming odds. They have addressed the following appeal to the French military authorities at Adana:

"The Turkish forces under Kemal have besieged us on all sides. They have distributed arms to all the Turkish villages in the neighborhood. The situation is critical. If you do not dispatch to us reinforcements and munitions we shall die after having gloriously resisted to the end. We are fighting to keep aloft the French flag, and this flag can save us if you will come to our rescue, otherwise you shall hear their cry of agony as 6,000 Armenians of Hadjin are wiped out in blood.

(Signed) "KAYIAN, TOHAYAN.

D.2

The New York Times, November 2, 1920:
"Turks Take Hadjin"

This is a report of the final Turkish takeover of Hadjin. The statement that "American personnel" had been forced the prior June to flee their orphanage, school, and hospital aligns with Mary's narrative.

Turks Take Hadjin, Slay 10,000 Armenians; Town Had Withstood Siege for Eight Months

LONDON, Nov. 1.—The Armenian town of Hadjin has been captured by Turkish Nationalists who have massacred the inhabitants, numbering 10,000, according to a despatch to the Armenian Bureau in London.

These Armenians had been holding out against the attacking forces since March last.

Hadjin is a town in the Cilician Taurus, 100 miles north and a little east of Adana, an important point on the Aleppo division of the Bagdad Railway. After the massacre of Marash in January, Mustapha Kemal Pasha, the leader of the Turkish Nationalists, with headquarters at Angora, sent raids against Hadjin, Orfa and Aintab, all within a radius of 50 miles. Urfa was practically wiped out, Aintab was relieved on March 28 by a French column operating from Adana, but the column failed to reach hadjin, which was apparently left to its fate.

The next news from this region came on October 4, when it was announced that General Gouraud, the French Commander-in-Chief in the East, would presently withdraw his troops beyond the River Dichinan, which, it was pointed out by the Armenian Bureau in London, would expose some 80,000 Armenians and hundreds of foreign refugees in Adana, Tarsus, and Mersina.

On the other hand, it was denied at the Paris War Office that Gouraud meditated any such extensive withdrawal, and it was said that an army of 40,000 Armenians had been drilled and mobilized at Adana, equipped with rifles and some heavy ex-Bulgarian guns sent over from Greece, and were ready to take the field against the Turkish Nationalists when Gouraud deemed the time propitious. It was added that one of their first objectives would be to relieve Hadjin.

Hadjin has been a centre of American relief work since the massacres of Armenians were begun in Turkey in 1915. Last June Turks attacked the orphanages, schools and hospitals operated in Hadjin by the Near East Relief and compelled the American personnel to leave the city, after they had been under fire in their buildings for three days. Administration of the relief work was turned over to local Armenians, but funds for its maintenance have been furnished by the Near East Relief.

D.3

The New York Times, November 5, 1920:
"Armenians Complain of French"

This is an editorial written by Armenian journalist, editor, and poet Arshag Mahdesian, accusing the French of interfering in Armenian Nationalist efforts in Cilicia, just after Hadjin fell to the Turks.

ARMENIANS COMPLAIN OF FRENCH

New York, Nov. 5, 1920

To the Editor of the New York Times:

In an editorial article entitled "Economic Partition," you contend that Armenians lean "toward the French when French troops are at hand as a protection against the Turks. When the Armenians have to shift for themselves, as they have had to do lately, there is no particular love for France among them."

The lack of love on the part of the Armenians toward France is not due to the fact that France leaves the Armenians to shift for themselves, but to the fact that she does not. Since the withdrawal of the British troops from Cili-cia, the French military has resorted to every means in order to render self-defense by the Armenians against the Turks impossible.

Just the other day the dispatches from Europe announced that the Armenian city of Hadjin, Cilicia, which had withstood the assault of Kemalist hordes since March, was captured by the Turks because the French did not permit an Armenian rescuing party of soldiers to raise its siege. An official report received by the American Committee for Armenian Independence from the most Rev. Moushek Seropia, at Smyrna, reads in part:

"No sooner had the Turks signed the treaty of peace at Sèvres than the French military began to persecute the Armenians in Cilicia, and to hamper the activities of the Armenian National Union, which zealously upheld the national rights of the Armenians. The

French, in order to increase the majority of the Turkish population and to en-
courage the Kemalist hordes, resolved
to deport the 100,000 Armenian population of Cilicia, and to disarm the
Armenian soldiers.

"The French officers on the Board
of Emigration first notified the 14,000
Armenians in the refugee camps, who
were given the choice to be deported
either to Alexandretta, Chok-Merzi-
foun, Beirut, Smyrna, Constantinople
or Erivan. When the Armenian refugees refused to comply with this demand, the French officers threatened to
turn machine guns on them. Then the
Armenian National Union intervened
and the French postponed the execution of their orders.

"On Sept. 22, General Martin, the
military governor of Adana, invited the
members of the Armenian National
Union for a consultation. When the
members reached his office, General
Martin declared that they were all
under arrest, as they had opposed the
execution of the French orders for the
pacification of the country. Immediately the French gendarmes took
charge of them and rushed them in military automobiles to Karatash and
thence to Alexandretta. Soon after Captain Shishmanian, Commander of the
Armenian forces in Cilicia, was sum-
moned and informed that, on the order
of General Gouraud, he must depart
from Cilicia. He was forthwith placed
under arrest and taken to Karatash.

"After this glorious French victory
over the Armenians, the French, with
two regiments of infantry, six machine

guns and two armored automobiles,
surrounded the village of Akarja, where
the Armenians soldiers were stationed
on their way to succor Hadjin, still re-
sisting heroically the hordes of Mustapha Kemal. The French commander
informed the Armenian soldiers that
they must be disarmed and leave the
country. The Armenian soldiers submitted for fear they might furnish the
French with the excuse of an Armenian
insubordination. These Armenian soldiers who were disarmed and deported
were the same that had helped the
chivalrous French to vanquish the
Turks and occupy Cilicia."

The French policy has simply been
an effort to denude Cilicia of its Armenian population, which it regards as
an obstacle to the execution of the in-
famous Sykes-Picot pact, concluded
secretly, in May, 1916, and allotting
Cilicia, Sivas, Diarbekr and all the rest
of Western Armenia—now dubbed
with the fictitious name of Kurdistan—
to France.

The American relief workers reported long ago that the French forces
in Cilicia were endeavoring rather to
eliminate the Armenian element than to
defend them. When representative Armenians protested to General Gouraud
against the atrocities of the Turks, who
were being encouraged by the French
attitude, and demanded that the Armenians be protected or permitted to defend themselves, he replied brazenly
that the French were not in Cilicia to
defend the Armenians, but to help them
to emigrate to the provinces of Russian
Armenia. It was for the elimination of

the Armenian element that M. Picot went to Sivas and promised Mustapha Kemal the French support of his so-called Nationalist movement, and that the Kemalist marauding bands were accorded, amid loud cheers, the following eulogy by M. Aristide Briand in the French Chamber of Deputies:

"The Allies have told the Turks, 'Yes, you shall live,' and then, 'no, you shall not live,' and have thereby brought about the present situation in Asia Minor, where we are confronted by so-called brigand bands. Such bands, if they were acting in similar circumstances in France, would be hailed by Frenchmen as patriots."

In 1916, when the French forces were being depleted, the French Government, through its representative in Egypt, made arrangements with the leaders of the Armenian political parties for raising Armenian volunteers, and promised full political justice to Armenia. More than 10,000 Armenians fought the battles of France against the Germans and the Turks, distinguishing themselves with heroism. If great nations at times cannot shift for themselves, it is natural that the Armenians should expect some aid from those who during the war praised them as their "little ally."

ARSHAG MAHDESIAN

APPENDIX E

Excerpts from the Memoirs of Alice Clark and Blanche Eby

E.1:   Alice Keep Clark, *Letters from Cilicia* (Chicago: A. D. Wein-
       throp & Co., 1924), 113-23.

E.2:   Blanche Remington Eby, *At the Mercy of Turkish Brigands: A
       True Story* (New Carlisle, Ohio: Bethel Publishing Co., 1922),
       23-48.

E.1

From Alice Keep Clark's *Letters from Cilicia*, pp. 113-23

*The excerpted pages that follow feature Alice's comments on "the way
the French are handling matters in this region," in particular their
arming of Armenians, because of the relief workers' fears that Armenians would seek retribution for past violence. She also notes the absence of French troops, while in their place there are only "Armenians
in French uniforms." Alice also describes Armenians "practising warfare." Throughout this section, Alice narrates the approach of the Nationalists as they take neighboring towns and includes an account of
the massacres at Marash.*

WRITTEN BUT NOT SENT

February Third

So many rumors come to us that I have decided to keep a record of events which may be of interest to you later. I shall write nothing in my letters that will give you cause for alarm as you cannot help us whatever happens. Because this account, if you ever read it, will not go through the regular channels but will be handed to you, I shall tell you some things which I should not dare trust to the post on account of censorship. I have said little about the way the French are handling matters in this region. You know that they have been given control of Cilicia and their present policy is to supply weapons to the Armenians. It is a policy which seems to us most unwise, for the Armenians, smarting from past cruelty and injustice, are certain to take it out on the Turks when the opportunity offers. All through the fall and winter the Armenians have, by means of dramatic entertainments, kept their past sufferings vivid. The Turkish kai-

kaimakam

LETTERS   FROM   CILICIA

makam has been removed and an Armenian has
replaced him.

We have heard of some Turkish villages where
arms have been forcibly seized by Armenian gendarmes. All this creates unrest and friction. Word
has come to us that a great body of Turks is being
gathered together in the north under a leader
called Mustapha Kemal Pasha, who is determined
to drive the French out of the country. It is said
that Marash is being attacked. You will recall that
this city is four days' journey from us—about a
hundred and twenty miles—and our Hadjin people
are in a panic. They say, "We shall be the next."
Although the French are supposed to be protecting
Cilicia, not a French soldier has been sent to this
city to guard it although the French have filled all
the offices with their own appointees,—Armenians
in French uniforms—and the French flag has been
raised over the Gregorian school.

It is very cold and we have had much snow, so
that at present the mountain passes cannot be traveled but when the snow melts we shall see. It is
reported that even the Turkish women and boys
are being armed and our poor people feel that they
are doomed.

February Fourth

The bodvilli has tried telegraphing to Marash
—it is long since post has come from friends there
—*but*

[114]

LETTERS   FROM   CILICIA

—but no word gets through, so we are confirmed in our fears that that place is surrounded and cut off. This afternoon we got the horses out and rode over to the orphanage in the vank, carried on by the Armenian committee. The poor matron has lost so many members of her family in massacres that she has little hope that Hadjin will be spared. All this and the stories told on every side of past horrors is not especially cheering in view of our present situation. Fortunately we are so overwhelmed with work that we have little time to think of anything else. My children must have their new clothes made and their old ones patched. It is a mercy that the common task can almost fill the horizon.

February Sixth

We are told that in the region of Everek, the Turks are massing, with Hadjin as one of their chief objectives. A letter has come to us from Rear Admiral Bristol—our High Commissioner in Constantinople—reminding us that all Americans in Turkey must be absolutely neutral, siding with neither French nor Armenians. Groups of Armenians are constantly coming to the compound to discuss the sending of letters and telegrams. The French reply that there is no reason for fear—when the need arises, adequate protection will be provided.

February

L E T T E R S   F R O M   C I L I C I A

February Eighth

Edith has just been over to tell me of word that
has come from an Armenian village, far away on
the border of Cilicia, asking that the people be received and sheltered in Hadjin. It seems heartless
to refuse but with this city overcrowded—the people in many cases living in caves and holes in the
ground—seven thousand trying to live in the five
hundred houses that still stand, there is no room.

February Eleventh

I am writing this in the evening after a most
terrible day. About nine o'clock this morning, two
Armenians, almost unconscious from cold and exhaustion, came to our gate. Their story was this—
the Americans in Marash, which had been cut off
from the world for several weeks, sent a courier
with word of their condition to Hadjin. He
reached Zeitoon but would go no further. Lots
were cast among the Zeitoonlu for two men to
continue the journey. The ones who drew the fatal
papers said, "To go is death, to stay is death," and
so, traveling only at night and by way of the mountain peaks, almost perishing with cold, they came
to us. They had been on the road six nights. They
had a paper saying the bearers were to be paid
twenty gold pounds. The message they brought
was in the form of a telegram and read as follows—"The Turks and the French are fighting.
The

LETTERS FROM CILICIA

The French, who are fighting from our compound, are distinctly on the defensive. Many Christians in the city have been killed, some of our orphans wounded. We are short of food. Send word to Arnold and Bristol Constantinople and American Consul Aleppo." This was signed by the relief director of Marash. It seems so strange and pitiful to think that Marash, a large city, should be seeking help from little Hadjin, the most inaccessible place where relief work is being done. However we still have telegraphic communication and as soon as the message could be taken to the station it was on its way—we hope it will not be tampered with.

These same men brought a letter to our bodvilli from the one in Marash, which told of the cutting down of his young wife and two little children by the Turks. You in America may know more of conditions in the interior than we but the danger seems near. We four had a consultation in Edith's office. In my letter which went to you yesterday, I told you of the arrival of Mr. Seeley, a relief worker from Adana who came for a few days' visit and to bring blankets and cloth. He urged us to go to Adana while the road is still open. With one accord, we three said, "No, our place is here." It is desirable for Mr. Seeley to return to Adana for he can present our situation to the authorities and we want him to go at once. Edith and I talked together after the others had left. Edith said, "I

feel

LETTERS   FROM   CILICIA

feel that it is quite possible that six weeks from
now we shall not be living." We quietly face that
thought for we know that if, by leaving now, we
could save our lives, we should lose our souls. Life
seems very sweet to me and I long to see you all
again—but if the end is to come here in Turkey
and at the hands of the Turks, then I must believe it
is God's plan for me. If death here is to be my lot,
then I pray that I may meet it with courage high.
Some time ago, I read some verses in the Congrega-
tionalist that moved me and I cut out the bit.   I
am going to copy it here, for at this moment, it
gives me comfort.

> "In pastures green? Not always; sometimes He
> Who knoweth best, in kindness leadeth me
> In weary ways, where heavy shadows be.
>
> And by still waters? No, not always so,
> Oftimes the heavy tempests round me blow,
> And o'er my soul the waves and billows go.
>
> But when the storms beat loudest and I cry
> Aloud for help, the Master standeth by,
> And whispers to my soul, 'Lo, it is I'.
>
> Lo, where He leads me, I can safely go,
> And in the blest hereafter, I shall know
> Why, in his wisdom, He has led me so."

I am writing a note to Mr. B——, which will
go with Mr. Seeley to Adana and then by courier
to Constantinople, from where it can be sent by
British post. This note contains a sealed letter to
you, which, when there is reasonable proof that I
am not living, will be given to you.

February

[118]

L E T T E R S   F R O M   C I L I C I A

February Twelfth

Mr. Seeley left us today and although it was absolutely the right thing for him to go, we felt somewhat forlorn as he disappeared down the road. We hope that the food requisition we sent by him can be filled and sent to us while there is still opportunity.

February Fifteenth

As my cold continues and I cough almost incessantly I have again taken to my bed so that what news filters in is brought to my room. Some of the girls who have been working hard for a concert to be given the last of March came over to talk. They are much depressed and Leah said, "What is the use? We shall all be killed by that time." In one way or another all the children hear about the threatened trouble and yesterday dear chubby little Vahan declared, "If the Turks come to cut off my head I shall just run away." Poor little things, the name Islam makes them tremble. Of course there are many friendly Turks who have never had any sympathy for the outrages perpetrated on the Armenians. In many cases Turks have hidden and protected Armenians but when danger threatens it is hard for them to remember that there is such a thing as a good Turk. As I look from my window I see an Armenian most picturesquely dressed. He is a soldier and a member of the group of twenty men who are on guard

on

[119]

LETTERS   FROM   CILICIA

on one of the peaks above us. The air is sharp and
he wears a white bashlek, a kind of hood made by
the Circassians, the ends of which, after being
crossed in front, tie again at the back. With his
many bands of cartridges and his gun he looks for-
midable. We must be absolutely neutral so we
have refused to contribute money toward defense
but we have satisfied ourselves that it is right to
lend blankets to keep the men warm as they watch.

*   *   *   *   *

A messenger has just come with letters from
Adana urging us to leave—the thought being that
in case the Turks come and a massacre follows
we shall be powerless to save our orphans. We see
no reason for altering our decision and we shall
stay with the terrified people, knowing that our
presence is a comfort to them. We have had some
parties for the children to turn their thoughts from
their fright. It is a satisfaction to do this for it
takes so little to give them pleasure.

February Eighteenth
Still no real knowledge of conditions. Naturally the people constantly talk of past suffering.
Mariam, one of my sewing women, has a sadder
look than ever in her eyes as she thinks of her three
children who died of starvation as they traveled
the exile's road to Der Zor and of her husband who
was buried alive. How many Rachels there are
weeping

LETTERS   FROM   CILICIA

weeping for their children! Elisa, just at the point
of graduation, so loyal and right minded, cannot
forget that ten years ago her father was cut down
in his own bake oven in the village of Fekke by
the Turks. It is difficult to feel optimistic but,
because of the pathetic faith that the native people
have in Americans, we must smile while our hearts
are sad. I have been looking over some papers I
brought with me from home and I came across a
a copy of that fine old Lutheran hymn that we so
love. Some of the lines seem to fit well into the
past, present and future of this mistreated nation.

"The vast unnumbered throngs that sway,
Around the throne in white array,
All swinging palms and singing psalms
Of vict'ry: Who are they?
They are the ransom'd hosts that from
Temptation, cross and martyrdom
Have come to meet at Jesus' feet
In the eternal home.
And there array'd in cleans'd attire
Their anthems sing to harp and lyre,
With cherubim and seraphim
In heav'n's celestial choir.

"While here on earth their hearts were sad,
But see them now, surpassing glad,
Triumphant face the throne of grace,
In regal garments clad.
In trials and misfortunes they
Had none their sorrows to allay;
But there above, the God of love
Has wiped their tears away.

They

LETTERS   FROM   CILICIA

They now enjoy the Sabbath rest
And paschal banquet of the blest,
At festal board, where Christ, their Lord,
Himself is host and guest."

February Twenty-second

This afternoon while I was writing I heard a
tap on my door and found that the bodvilli had
come to say goodbye. It has just been decided
that he shall go to Adana to put in a personal plea
for help for Hadjin. His companions are the Gregorian bishop and the head of the Gregorian
school. What they can accomplish is uncertain but
it is worth trying.

February Twenty-sixth

No authentic word has come to us but there is
a rumor that the men on their way to Adana were
attacked. We do not know their fate. In the
meantime fear increases.

February Twenty-seventh

We have two Moslem girls in the school, Ayesha about twenty years old who was divorced for
no cause by her husband and is anxious to get an
education, hoping to be able to teach, and a dear
little girl, Jennet who is eleven or twelve. Today
both girls were brought by their mothers with the
request that they stay all the time at the school.
The feeling toward all Moslems is not good—there
are about three hundred in Hadjin—and these two
mothers

[122]

LETTERS   FROM   CILICIA

mothers fear for their daughters. Edith has given them permission to come tonight.

February Twenty-eighth

This afternoon I looked out toward a small level place in the little valley on my side of the compound and saw a group of Armenians practising warfare. They would advance a short way, then throw themselves on their faces, bringing their guns into position. Again and again they did this. For hundreds of years the Turks have forbidden the use of weapons to the Armenians so that now they are doing their best to prepare themselves to meet the enemy. It is a pathetic sight to see the men in this mountain pocket doing what they can to protect the city. A rather lawless band of Armenians called gamavoors has drifted into the place. They are men from the region of Erzroom and Everek, who were driven into exile in 1915, and found nothing but ruined homes to greet them on their return. Having neither families nor homes they are ready to sell their services for a small sum to any place needing help. Their leader is a man who fought under the great Antranik in the Caucasus. In many ways the coming of these men is bad for the city for they have gained control of the place and, despite the wishes of many of the citizens, are harassing the Moslems of Hadjin and those in the surrounding villages. It was one of these men who frightened Ayesha's mother.

March

[123]

E.2

From Blanche Eby's
***At the Mercy of Turkish Brigands,* pp. 23-48**

*The following excerpted pages come towards the beginning of
Blanche's text and describe the 1915 deportations and exile. Blanche's
memoirs are written in the style of historical fiction. As noted in the
Introduction, she refers to herself and her fellow relief workers using
the names given to them by the Nationalist soldiers (e.g., Mary is "the
Doctor Lady"; Alice Clark is "the Tall One.") Early in her text, she
describes "The Trail of Death" and "The Desert Life" by recounting
the personal stories of survivors she knew and with whom she spoke.
Among them was Menas Effendi, who appears in all three memoirs.*

CHAPTER III

The Trail of Death

ROUND about the city rose the great mountains, their tops blanketed with filmy clouds. The morning sun was just kissing the peaks and turning all into rose vapour. The city, nestling in the narrow valley at their base, still lay in shadow. But the minds of the inhabitants were filled with gloomier shadows than those cast by the mountains.

The spur of one mountain penetrated into the narrow valley, and the city rambled part way up this. There were thousands of little bee-hive houses, perched and clinging, and numberless narrow streets, steep and perilous, zigzagged up the mountainside. At the foot of this mountain spur the canyon began to narrow and here, before the government buildings, hundreds of Armenian families were lined up. From time to time, a few days apart, they were being sent out in parties of about one thousand each.

What a heart-rending scene it was! The faces of the younger men were white and set as chiselled marble. Dumb distress twisted the weatherbeaten features of the middle-aged, while their tones carried all the inflections of despair. The weeping of the children and the wailing of the women mingled with the shouts of the soldiers, the creaking of the oxcarts, and the cruel blows from the whips of the gendarmes.

Poor little orphans from the mission were among the number. Their hearts were chilled with fear.

23

AT THE MERCY OF TURKISH BRIGANDS

Here and there a girl, losing control of her overburdened heart, gave way to the strong tide of her feelings sobbing out, "Oh, I am so anxious and fearful about the future." The women and girls veiled themselves that they might escape the gaze of their brutal guards. They were in an agonizing state of apprehension, for they feared that the men would all be killed, and they themselves kidnapped along the way. Blank despair was in their faces, and a terrible hopelessness sounded in the broken, quivering tones of their farewell.

In describing it to the writer, the Vartabed, the Armenian Bishop of Hadjin, said: "What a sad and black Friday that was! It was the day of Hadjin's ruin; a day of suffering and agony to my unfortunate people; a day of barbaric Turkish atrocities which no power of man's language can describe. Two hundred soldiers formed up on each side of the road to guard the exiles on their journey. They started out with slow, unsteady step, turning to take a last look at their deserted homes, and to cast a last glance upon the graves of their fathers, while the unmerciful soldiers were terrorizing them to make them move faster. As they crossed the bridge outside the city, a peculiar feeling took possession of them. They wondered if they would ever return over that bridge again, or whether they were marching to a distant graveyard in the desert of Horan, or in the River Euphrates. No pen will ever be able to describe the diabolical horrors committed by a government existing in this glorious, civilized (?) century."

The same evening this Vartabed received the following letter from one of the exiles:

24

THE TRAIL OF DEATH

"Shar-shar, June 4th, 1915.

"My Dear Bishop:—

"We are now in Shar-shar, which, as you know, is only a distance of ten kilometers from Hadjin. Yet it seems more than ten thousand kilometers away as we have no longer hope to live or to be able to return to our homes.

"In traveling this short distance many are ill and exhausted. What will be the final result? How many of us will ever reach our destination? We are simply marching to our graves. Our party is guarded by twenty-five soldiers in front, twenty-five in our rear; seventy-five on our right, and seventy-five on our left. The ever-ready lash is at hand to scourge all who get out of line.

"In this short distance we have buried a child, and we expect, as we proceed on our journey, a great many more of our number will collapse. Nevertheless, our banishment is even a relief, for at least we are free from the brutal Commandant who made life a misery for us during our last months in Hadjin. It would be a still greater relief if the soldiers were not accompanying us. Our women are so terrified at their conduct. They act more like fiends than human beings.

"Farewell, our dear father Bishop. We beg of you to remember us in your prayers to the merciful Father above, and we pray that you may have His help in your lonely situation.

"Your transported and unhappy flock."

Most of the Armenians lived in the highlands of Anatolia and Cilicia. To be driven down into the

25

AT THE MERCY OF TURKISH BRIGANDS

Mesopotamian plain, with its semi-tropical climate, meant terrible suffering for these mountaineers. It also meant suffering for the Turks who were left behind, for the greater part of the trade and commerce carried on in the interior had been in the hands of the Armenians, who have a high intellect and superior business ability. If the Turk were not so envious he could see that they are really a great blessing to his country. They were the carpenters, the tanners, the weavers, the shoemakers, the merchants, the blacksmiths of the country; and in driving them out the Turks failed to see that they were leaving themselves in a helpless state. The following winter many of them had to go without shoes, as they did not know how to make them. Their clothing fell into rags, and there were no Armenians to weave cloth for new garments.

It was this remarkable talent for business that excited the envy of the Turks, for many Armenians, by their industry, had become people of property. The deportations now gave the Turk the opportunity of gaining possession of this property. To the Turk's way of thinking this was not stealing, for were not the Moslems the chosen ones of Allah, and had Allah himself not given them this opportunity?

Yet, while it is true that the Turk usually had no regard either for the life or property of the Armenian, there were a few instances, though only few, where they respected both. Some Moslems did try to save their Christian neighbors, offering them shelter in their own homes, though in vain. The uniform commands from Constantinople were carried out with scrupulous exactitude on the part of the local authori-

26

THE TRAIL OF DEATH

ties all over the country. In many cases the time allowed was too short to permit them to dispose of their possessions at even a small per cent of their value. Some were not allowed to make any provision at all for the journey. Others were dragged out of bed without even sufficient clothing. The women of one village, who were at the washtub when the order came, were compelled to leave their clothes in the wash and start out just as they were, barefoot and half-clad.

Under the hot summer sun many a caravan proceeded through the Taurus Mountains, and out over the burning Cilician plain. Those who have had no experience of travel in Turkey cannot imagine the suffering and fatigue entailed by such a journey. Many died on the way from starvation, thirst, or abuse. Bands of Kurd brigands and Moslem peasants from villages along the route fraternized with the gendarmes and were allowed to plunder the exiles. Even the clothes were stolen from the backs of many, and some, women among the number, were compelled to travel absolutely naked under the burning sun. Powerless to prevent it, fathers and mothers witnessed the violation of their daughters. Women, girls, and children were carried off to be enslaved into a life of degradation.

Among the great company was a prominent family, the Manasajians from Hadjin. Mehron, the youngest of the four brothers, had taught for years in the mission school. Later he had gone to the American College at Beyrout and had learned to be a druggist. On his return he had opened a drug store in Hadjin, and, with his newly-acquired knowledge and his store

27

AT THE MERCY OF TURKISH BRIGANDS

of medicines, he was ever ready to assist the missionaries in caring for any of the orphans who fell ill.

He had married a refined young teacher from the mission whose father, a native pastor, had been killed in a previous massacre. They had one child, an exceptionally bright and attractive baby boy.

The sun shone down on them with fierce, merciless rays. All day long they had marched over the desolate, sun-baked plain. Not a living thing was in sight: not a tree or a blade of grass. The exiles were weak from hunger, frantic with thirst, and had reached the stage where their lips were dry and cracking open, tongues swollen, throats parched, and brains on fire with misery. Life had become so excruciating that it is small wonder that a few were bereft of their reason. Many dropped by the way, glad that for them the awful nightmare of suffering was over. The great vultures hovered above their heads, flapping their wings impatient to devour their prey.

Toward the evening the caravan reached a valley where there was flowing water, and camped for the night a short distance from the spring. What agonies of thirst they had endured during the long day on the dusty plains! Now they heard the gurgling music of sweet water as it rippled over the pebbles just across the narrow valley. How it sparkled and flowed in copious abundance before their aching eyes! The baby stretched out its little hands toward it and cooed in glee.

But these poor people were treated worse than cattle by their brutal guards, who took a fiendish delight in keeping them without water.

"Have mercy on our children," cried Manoog, the

28

THE TRAIL OF DEATH

eldest of the Manasajian brothers. "We will forego the privilege, desperate as our need is, if only you will allow our little ones to drink of this water." But the murderous gendarmes were deaf to this and every piteous plea from the parents. They laughed at all their supplications during the evening, utterly unmoved by the tears of the children, and no one was allowed to drink water there. As a result death soon robbed Mehron of his beautiful boy, and many another parent mourned the loss of little ones.

The miseries with which the exiles were afflicted are indescribable. The result was seen in the line of corpses that marked each caravan route. And what a cry of agony went up from the survivors, especially from the women. Under cover of the night unthinkable deeds were committed by the gendarmes, and many women died as a result of these outrages.

The soldiers meant to complete the work of annihilation, and few of these exiles would ever return. Wild Arab bands were allowed to sweep down upon them, and again and again awful scenes of loot and massacre ensued. Many were trampled to death, while others were slaughtered with merciless ruthlessness. "Where is your Christ now?" the pitiless captors would jeer. "Why does He not come and save you?"

Girls were sold along the route, or carried away by force. What prospect of a decent life was there for these beautiful young women? What hope of an honorable marriage in the distant future? In this struggle for life and honor many a girl was forced to make her decision: she must either go into a harem or commit suicide. No other choice lay before her.

29

AT THE MERCY OF TURKISH BRIGANDS

Some of the women threw themselves down from the rocks into the Euphrates to save their honor—some of these were young mothers with infants in their arms. Others carried poison in their pockets to use if necessary.

No attempt will be made here to mention in detail the awful atrocities committed by the inhuman guards during the exile. They are too horrible. The reader would not care to hear them. It has frequently been said that the gloomy reports of the sufferings of the Armenians must be grossly exaggerated. But those of us who have lived in Turkey know that the half has never been told. The refinements of physical cruelties practiced on the Armenians could not be printed; they are so revolting that they would not be read if printed.

30

CHAPTER IV

The Desert Life

A SCORCHING sun blazed down on the vast, shadow-less plain. There was nothing in sight to cheer the traveler or inspire him with fresh hope. No tree relieved the weary monotony, no sheltering rock, no sparkling brook—nothing but a dreary desert waste under a burning sky.

The survivors were still being remorselessly driven on to a lingering death. After crossing the Cilician plain they had reached Aleppo, a city which lies in an oasis of the desert. The malarial swamps beyond the city were given to the first comers. But soon the place did not suffice for the caravans that continued to arrive week after week. Orders were then given for them to proceed to Der-el-Zor, a place six days' journey to the southeast in the Arabian desert.

Among the survivors was Menas Effendi. His family was still intact. This was probably due in part to the fact that the missionaries had given him some money. With this he had been able at times to purchase food and water at exorbitant prices. They had also given him their Midily (a Turkish word used for a small pony) and his wife, Markareet Hanum, with the baby and smaller children, had been able to ride part of the time.

They found the melancholy of the vast plains oppressive. It lay like a weight on their hearts, and Menas Effendi was experiencing a dreariness of spirit

31

AT THE MERCY OF TURKISH BRIGANDS

that was rare in him. In a few days they would reach Der-el-Zor, and he was filled with strange forebodings of coming evil. It was already a well-known fact that few exiles who were sent to Der-el-Zor ever returned. The caravan was now on its way to this terrible place of death. One man was heard to say, "If anything further happens to us I shall say there is no God."

"How can you speak thus?" asked Menas Effendi. "I do not feel that way about our sufferings. For my part I shall never finish telling of the many, many times God has delivered us already. If I do not survive, I shall believe that God knows best, and shall say, 'The will of the Lord be done.'" Undergirded by the omnipotent hand of God, Menas Effendi found rest of mind and heart in His will during these months, which must have tested every atom of faith in his being.

When the warm tints of sunset were flooding the western sky, they saw a large party of Arabs approaching. Seeing the exiles, the Arabs rejoiced, for it afforded them one more opportunity to rob and carry away plunder.

Uttering frightful yells, the Arabs attacked the exiles and began carrying off women and girls. Markareet Hanum slipped on Menas Effendi's long cape so the Arabs would not know that she was a woman, and began burying all their money—two gold pounds —under a shrub.

Menas Effendi did what he could to resist the Arabs, and was able to rescue five women. All the exiles who could, had run away, after first putting their money in saddlebags and giving it to Menas

THE DESERT LIFE

Effendi, asking him to bring it later if he escaped. He now drew off to one side in the bushes and knelt to pray.

"Rise up and take a long stick from these bushes in your hand," he heard a voice saying to him. He answered: "But, Lord, the Arabs number four hundred, and I am only one man. What good would a stick be in this case? They would think I meant to beat them with it, and that would make them angry."

But, in spite of his protests the voice persisted. He rose, and taking a long stick in his hand he marched out toward the Arabs, who were still busy gathering up the plunder. To his intense surprise, when they saw him coming, they took to their heels and fled.

The ten exiles, who alone remained, gazed in awe at the fleeing enemy. The Arabs, though they had revolvers which they had been firing off from time to time, had no rifles among them. When they saw Menas Effendi approaching them in the dusk, they thought the long stick in his hand was a rifle, and ran in fear for their lives. "It was then," remarked Menas Effendi afterward, "that I first began to understand the verse, 'One shall chase a thousand.' I realized afresh what a wonderful privilege it was to have God himself deal with a situation which was altogether beyond human strength."

Next morning he spent two or three hours gathering up the goods, which the Arabs had dropped in their hasty flight, and loading them on the animals. Later in the day he overtook the Armenians who had escaped, and handed their possessions over to them.

"You might have kept some of these things," said

33

AT THE MERCY OF TURKISH BRIGANDS

one. "We would have been none the wiser, for we would have thought that the Arabs took them."

"That is true," said Menas Effendi in reply. "But if I had, my heart would have been full of greed and covetousness. I could not have prayed, and God would not have delivered us."

In a few days they reached Der-el-Zor. "This," said Menas Effendi, in relating the story to the author afterward, "was the most dreaded place of all. Eighty thousand Armenians lost their lives in the horrors that were enacted here. Let me relate the one about the Death Pit to you."

"I do not know," he began, "how this awful pit happened to be there. It looked as though some immense body had fallen from the sky, making a deep hole in the ground. The pit was one hundred and fifty feet deep.

"Imagine the scene if you can. A great field with tents scattered all over it. In these tents at that time there were over one thousand exiles in the last stages of sorrow and anguish of mind. On one side flowed the River Euphrates, and beside it was this strange pit.

"The Moslem soldiers—Turks, Kurds, Arabs, and Circassians—were going about among the tents giving orders for the people to prepare themselves. At the appointed time the soldiers would come, gather together one hundred of the exiles and escort them down to this pit, where they threw them in one by one. They then returned for the second hundred, and threw them in also. Back and forth they went all day at this awful task, until the pit was filled right up to the top.

"Those underneath soon smothered. Those on top

34

THE DESERT LIFE

lived a long time: some lived ten days. The soldiers, who were guarding the mouth of the pit that none be allowed to escape, were sitting around eating and drinking day after day. To them it was sport to tantalize the people in the pit by showing them the food, and calling out: 'See! Here is food. We are eating. Here is water. We are drinking.'

"The poor creatures in the pit got to such a desperate strait at length that some ate their own children. Dreadful as this was, some even quarreled with their neighbors over these gruesome meals. At this time one of the children said to her mother, 'Mother, when my turn comes, and you eat me, please do not give any of my body to that stingy woman, who refused to give you some of her child today.'

"Only one person is known to have escaped from that pit of death. With the clothes already torn from her body, one godly woman, whose home was in Marash, and whom I know well, managed to crawl out at night and, skilfully evading the soldiers, fled away in the darkness."

When the caravan, in which Menas Effendi and his family were, reached Der-el-Zor they found the place filled with refugees. So many thousands could not be disposed of even by death pits. They were, therefore, sent on to wander again in the deserts until such time as those vast regions of death should claim them.

A few days elapsed before the order for them to start out was given. Typhus was raging among the exiles here, and Markareet Hanum, prompted by her kind, generous heart, had gone from tent to tent, during the time of their waiting in Der-el-Zor, ministering to the suffering ones.

35

AT THE MERCY OF TURKISH BRIGANDS

As a result she contracted the disease herself, and was feeling ill when the caravan started out. Her husband, Menas Effendi, placed her tenderly upon the Midily (pony) and did what he could to ease her suffering.

It was a huge caravan of eleven thousand souls. Mosul, situated on the Tigris River, near the ancient ruins of Nineveh, was their destination. It was ordinarily a journey of ten days across the desert that lies between the Euphrates and Tigris Rivers.

Owing to his superior intellect and business ability, Menas Effendi had been given charge of the records and the accounts for this great caravan. It seems that though the meager rations doled out at times to the exiles was not enough to sustain life, yet the government kept strict account of it; also a record of the number of exiles that left with each caravan, and the number of survivors that reached each new destination. In this way they were able to ascertain, from time to time, how the murder of the Armenian nation was progressing, and how much the process was costing the Ottoman Government.

Markareet Hanum looked out over the immense desolation before them: the white, dust-filled road, the glaring sun, the bodies of the fallen, and the great birds of prey hovering in the vault above them. A cloud of dust floated back from the caravan and faded away in the hazy distance behind them. They were passing through a region of silence and death. The borders of the road were strewn with bleached bones —mute witnesses of the sufferings of those who had already passed this way and succumbed to starvation, thirst, and fatigue.

36

THE DESERT LIFE

"I shall not recover from this illness," she said, at last, to her husband. "I feel that I am going to die. You must not worry, for it is better so. Think of the endless miseries I shall escape, and remember that heaven is awaiting me. There is only one thing that keeps troubling me." Here her voice broke in a sob. "How can I leave my baby? She is weak and ailing. I wish that she might be buried in the same grave with me."

Markareet Hanum grew steadily worse, and when the caravan halted for the night it was evident that she could not last long. While she could yet speak, she called those whom she knew to her side, and, giving them godly counsel and advice, urged them to be true to Jesus, their Lord, to the very end.

Through the night Menas Effendi ministered tenderly to his dying wife, and toward morning she passed away. Crushing down his grief, he set about digging a grave for the form of his loved one. As the caravan was about to start out, he sought and obtained permission from the gendarmes to remain behind one hour in order to bury his wife. Placing the body in the hastily dug grave, he uttered a prayer from his bleeding heart to his All-wise and Ever-kind Father, who had done all things well. No man could lose a loved companion and bend his head more submissively to the blow than Menas Effendi.

His work was not more than half finished when a band of wild Arabs, uttering fiendish yells, swept down upon him. He was, therefore, compelled to flee for his life, leaving the grave only half filled in. Alas, what tragedies, more cruel than any recorded in books, entered the lives of these exiles!

37

AT THE MERCY OF TURKISH BRIGANDS

The caravan was soon swallowed up in the immense desert spaces. Journeying on without any definite aim, they felt as though they were vowed to some eternal pilgrimage over the vast solitudes and wastes of earth. Though they were far out on the desert, yet in the dim distance, on the left, stretched a range of mountains. In and out, round about, up through the edge of the mountains and back over the desert they were dragged, again and again, by their cruel executioners.

In the intense pain of this wandering life, they lived and moved as one in a dream. There was nothing to look forward to: nothing but a lingering death. They had no opportunity to bathe even their hands and face, no change of clothing, and little to eat. In his heart Menas Effendi was thanking God for taking Markareet and sparing her the tortures of this final trip.

Now and then a cry of despair swept moaningly across the desert waste. The exiles were dying by the thousand along the route. In agony of soul a mother, as many another had done, watched her child reel and stumble from hunger and exhaustion. She placed it beside a withered shrub, hoping that it would be content to remain there, peacefully, until its soul passed away. But, as the caravan receded in the distance, the child with an agonized wail over being left behind, struggled weakly to its feet, and staggered after its mother, falling ever and anon, but rising again in a last vain attempt to follow.

There was a wild look in the eyes of the mother as she listened to the despairing cry of the deserted one. She, like many others, was compelled to abandon her

38

THE DESERT LIFE

child because it could walk no farther, and she never knew whether it died of hunger, whether some kind-hearted Moslem traveler, in passing that way soon after, took pity on it and carried it home with him, or whether it was devoured that night by the wild beasts.

Thus, from time to time, both children and adults were left by the roadside, too feeble to move on. Agonized mothers, almost demented with grief, threw their infants away, unable to carry them farther. Women, in the last stages of pregnancy, were driven along under the lash. Many were delivered on the road, and, being hurried along without mercy, died of hemorrhage soon after.

The gendarmes had appointed Menas Effendi to superintend the cooking of their meals. One, who was somewhat charitably inclined, became his friend. After all, these soldiers were only obeying orders from Constantinople, and occasionally one was found who took no pleasure in this death-dealing job. This gendarme, who became his friend, sold him some water and some food, secretly, every night. He had to pay eighty cents for each cupful of water. It was filthy and impure, but Menas Effendi strained it through his handkerchief and boiled it under cover of the darkness while he cooked the soldiers' food. He was trying desperately to keep his children alive, especially the baby, and in some way—God only knows how—he managed to do it.

He knew that the lives of these little ones had long been hanging on a slender thread. If the burning thirst and fatigue of the day should take his year-old baby Florence and little three-year-old Zelia—that was the fear that haunted him each day. He knew

AT THE MERCY OF TURKISH BRIGANDS

the uncertainty of life, even for a day. Yet he kept his firm trust in God, his brave reliance on the Unseen amid all the terrors and horrors of the seen. His faith in God never failed him. Through it all a strange hopefulness inspired him, and he was able to cheer many another fainting heart, encouraging them with his own brave trust in God.

A few more weeks of indescribable agony passed, and the morning of the forty-fourth day dawned. Far away like an ocean the sandy desert still stretched on every hand. The sun rose fiery red, like a ball of molten metal, over the vast lonely sweep. The long forenoon passed.

Surely, thought the exiles, they must be nearing Mosul! Eyes scanned the horizon with desperate gaze, searching for a cool, green oasis, but there was none in sight—nothing but burning stretches of sand. With no breeze to temper the heat during the day, the sun's rays fell on their heads like a blast from a furnace. The awfulness of the desolation: the horror of the distances over which, it seemed, they must march endlessly, lay like a pall on their spirits.

Now, as they looked out across the boundless expanse, they saw what appeared to be a green oasis. It remained there, for some time, before their tired eyes with tantalizing distinctness. In their imagination a vision rose: a vision of the surcease of sorrow, and sweet forgetfulness in some haven of rest and safety.

Hope put new energy into their lagging footsteps. They were hastening joyously toward it when suddenly it disappeared. The thing, which they were so ardently following after, like so many of the things

THE DESERT LIFE

in our world today, was a mirage—an empty nothing: a radiantly beautiful, attractive, alluring *nothing*.

Many of the exiles cried aloud and wept in their bitter disappointment. The unsympathetic soldiers laughed and jeered. The sun seemed to have renewed its fierceness as it blistered their skin and scorched their eyeballs: even it seemed to laugh and mock at them also in its burning fury, telling them that before another day their bones would be added to the number already whitening the desert waste.

Yet the Armenians are a hardy race, with extraordinary vitality, and some survived. Toward the close of the following day—the forty-fifth day—the Mesopotamian desert town of Mosul came into view. The weary exiles saw its many mosques standing out in bold relief against the horizon. The vegetation of this oasis was unutterably refreshing to their eyes after the heat and glare of the waterless regions.

As the caravan completed its long death-route it presented a pitiable aspect. The fleshless bodies of the exiles were so thin that the bones could be seen beneath the brown skin. Only a patchwork of rags covered their bodies. Out of that great company of eleven thousand souls only twenty-five hundred remained alive to enter Mosul.

Menas Effendi went at once to give his report to the Vali (the Governor of the province), who was filled with rage when he heard that so many had survived the terrible zig-zag journey from Der-el-Zor. He gave orders that the caravan turn back at once and return to Der-el-Zor.

"Have mercy, Your Excellency!" begged Menas Effendi. "Why prolong our misery further? The

41

AT THE MERCY OF TURKISH BRIGANDS

Tigris flows conveniently by. Take us out here and throw us into the river. It were so much kinder than to send us back again."

Pleading long with the Governor for mercy, the best Menas Effendi could do was to secure a compromise. The fainting exiles obtained a few days' respite, and then were forced to move onward to a place six days' journey farther on.

Something about the bearing of Menas Effendi must have commended itself to the authorities, for, greatly to his surprise, he and his family were commanded to remain in Mosul. No doubt they thought he might be useful to them.

During the next three years the exiles who survived the deportations, which have been but faintly described in this narrative, dragged out a miserable existence. Thousands died of dysentery, typhus, and cholera. Every conceivable form of unmentionable atrocities were committed, with violent brutality and cruel heartlessness, by their tormentors. Many were put to the most awful forms of torture that the ingenious Moslem mind could devise.

Knowing that they would be robbed of everything that they possessed, the poor exiles, in desperation, sometimes swallowed their money in order to save it. But alas, the Turks soon discovered this and it led to further scenes of revolting hideousness. The poor victims were disembowelled while still alive: not by chance, but ripped with careful precision and their bowels searched for any gold or silver pieces which might have been swallowed. One of the Hadjin orphans, Vartavar, a young man of exceptionally fine

42

THE DESERT LIFE

physique, who was Athletic Instructor to the younger boys, was killed in this way.

There is no desire on the part of the writer to prolong this tale of agony. The narrative has therefore been confined to the more ordinary horrors, while the exceedingly hideous and appalling physical cruelties —refinements of Turkish atrocities so revolting that one cannot even bear to hear them mentioned—have been purposely avoided.

The bitter, undying hatred of the Turk for all Christians is born of religious fanaticism. No amount of education or civilization will ever rid him of this feeling. He is precisely the same as when the wild hordes swept over Ásia Minor from Central Asia conquering Egypt, Arabia, Northern Africa, and the Balkan States. Five hundred years of contact with the civilization of Europe, since that time, has not changed the Turk. And no change can be expected until there is a change in his religion. The change must begin in his heart. He must accept the religion he so despises—the religion of Jesus Christ. That is the only remedy.

Turkey's eastern war zone ran through ancient Armenia, where, perhaps, half of the Armenians of the Turkish Empire were living. There was no need to deport these to get rid of them, for it was here that the Turkish and Russian battle lines swayed to and fro for so long, bringing death and destruction. Great numbers were massacred. Thousands of others fled across the Russian frontier.

The sufferings of these war refugees was terrible, and often equaled that of their brethren from Ana-

43

AT THE MERCY OF TURKISH BRIGANDS

tolia and Cilicia. Yet they were sustained by the thought that they were fleeing toward life and liberty while the exiles, even after reaching their destination, were never sure of food and shelter for several years.

Menas Effendi worked for a Moslem who gave him no wages, and did not always give him enough to eat. His three boys were constantly on the alert for odd jobs in the market place, in order to earn a few pennies. At times they were forced to gather grass for food. During the first year, Esther Mangurian, the Bible Woman, took care of his baby. Later she, like many others, succumbed to starvation.

Menas Effendi related many incidents of God's loving care for him during the exile. After his wife had been dead a little over a year he was living in a tent with his two youngest children, Zelia and Florence. One morning his master told him he must go away for the day on business, but he did not offer him any food for the journey. Both he and the children were very hungry. It grieved his father-heart to go away thus, so he went quietly into the tent and prayed for food for his hungry little ones.

Suddenly he felt very thirsty. He rose and decided that he would go down to the river for water. He started off, and when he reached the river he saw a large loaf of bread lying on the bank. No doubt it had dropped from the loads of some villagers who had passed that way with their donkeys.

Some may think all this happened accidentally, but Menas Effendi does not think so. Seizing the loaf, he hurried home with a heart that was well-nigh bursting with gratitude. To his hungry little girls he said: "See, little ones, God has sent us a loaf

44

THE DESERT LIFE

of bread from heaven. The God who fed Elijah—in the story I told you recently—still lives and is caring for us also."

The second year passed by. Menas Effendi was able to secure work from a Moslem citizen, who paid him a trifle for it. Each day, on his way to work, he was obliged to pass the home of a wealthy man. A poor woman came every day to this home to beg. Menas Effendi, who frequently overheard her pleading, felt like helping her, but he was scarcely earning enough to keep his own family alive. The rich man paid no heed to the woman, and finally she was on the verge of starvation. Menas Effendi could stand it no longer.

"I must help this poor creature, even if my little girls go hungry tonight," he said to himself, giving her all the money he had. As he continued on his way homeward he was wondering whether there was still sufficient time before dark for him to go outside the city and gather grass for food for their evening meal. Soon the children came running to meet him.

"Oh, Baba," cried Zelia, her eyes shining with the good news, "what do you think happened today? This afternoon we had a visitor who left us several loaves of bread." Jubilantly they took him by the hand and led him into their home.

"That is much more bread than my money would have bought," said Menas Effendi, gratefully, as he told the children the story of the poor starving woman. "You see, my darlings, how God takes care of His children when they obey His voice and sacrifice for others."

One more incident will suffice to show God's care

45

AT THE MERCY OF TURKISH BRIGANDS

for them in exile. It was during the third year. Zelia and Florence were crying. There was nothing to eat in the house, and Menas Effendi could find no work.

"Have patience, children. God will send us some food soon," he said. He did not know where the food was to come from, but he said it to give them comfort.

"But when, Baba, when will He send it? I am so hungry," cried Zelia in piteous tones that wrung the father's heart.

"Do not worry," he said, putting his arm about her comfortingly, "God will not forget."

Evening came and still no food. The children waited expectantly and Menas Effendi prayed silently, for he did not want them to lose their faith in God. One hour after another passed. The children were finding it hard to wait so long.

At last, after eight o'clock, there was a rap at the door, and a rich woman from the Protestant congregation appeared. In one hand she carried a bag of cracked wheat, and in the other hand a basket containing a piece of fresh meat and a loaf of bread.

She asked kindly whether they had any food in the house, but Menas Effendi, being a sensitive soul, evaded her question. She then began talking to the children, and from their innocent prattle soon discovered that they had been two days without food.

"Three days ago," she explained, "I felt impressed that I should call here with some food, but I did not do so. But tonight the call came so insistently that I felt I must come and see your condition for myself. Now I feel deeply grieved that I was so slow in obeying the Lord,"

46

THE DESERT LIFE

That night Menas Effendi and his family went to bed with renewed trust in the God who cares for His own.

The third year of exile passed slowly, amid indescribable hardships, for the Armenians. "When, oh when, will the Allies win the war and set us free?" was the constant thought of each. They could find little work in their wandering life among the peoples of a strange land. They longed to return to their former homes and occupations.

Many a family had been separated during the deportation days, the husband being marched off in one direction and the wife in another. Children were often sold or carried off along the way. Their only hope for reunion, or finding each other again, was to return to the old home town and await there the coming of loved ones who might, or might not, return. For this reason the Armenians prayed earnestly for the coming of the Allies. In those days the Turks used to say that one could easily tell how the war was progressing by watching the tell-tale faces of the Armenians.

The Armenian men were conscripted as soldiers, not to carry arms, but to work on the construction of roads and other manual labor. Menas Effendi and his eldest son, Panus, were made to work on the railroad. Even little Zelia, at her tender age, had to earn her own living by carrying small bags of earth on her back for the construction of the new road.

When at last the Allies were victorious in Mesopotamia, the joy of the exiles knew no bounds. As the conquering armies entered each city the Armenians strewed their pathways with flowers and

47

AT THE MERCY OF TURKISH BRIGANDS

greeted them with the wildest enthusiasm. The British soldiers seemed to them like angels from heaven come to open for them the door to liberty and freedom.

Many were sent to Egypt to be cared for in large concentration camps. Others remained in the towns occupied by the Allies. Relief workers now came and distributed food and clothing, and a new life opened up before the Armenian exiles.

Menas Effendi's second son, Yegvart, by his limited knowledge of English gained in the Hadjin mission school, attracted the attention of the British General, who engaged him as his cook. As he learned to open cans of beef and jams, and prepare meals from tinned goods, as well as ride by the general's side in an automobile—things which he had never seen before— he felt as though he were living in a happy dream.

48

APPENDIX F

Miscellaneous Personal Documents

F.1: Passport Application for Mary Watson Super, January 18, 1919, www.ancestry.com.

F.2: Excerpts from Charles V. Vickrey, *Teamwork: A Tribute and an Appeal*, ed. Mabell S. C. Smith (New York: Near East Relief National Headquarters Publication, 1924).

F.3: Letters and telegrams between Clark family and friends and government officials seeking information about the relief workers, June-July, 1920, National Archives and Records Administration.

F.4: Obituary of Mary Watson Super, *Main Line Chronicle*, Ardmore, PA, July 22, 1965.

F.1

Passport Application for Mary Watson Super, January 18, 1919

Note that on the application form the "Name of Country" designation is changed from Armenia to Turkey. "Purpose of Visit" includes "Nursing— Red Cross," and "Relief work" is added by hand.

Form for Native Citizen

UNITED STATES OF AMERICA.
State of *Pennsylvania*
County of *Philadelphia*

I, *Mary Watson Super (Single)*, a Native and Legal Citizen of the United States, hereby apply to the Department of State, at Washington, for a passport.

I solemnly swear that I was born at *Lower Merion Township*, in the State of *Pennsylvania*, on or about the *13th* day of *June, 1882*, that my *father, Jacob Super,* was born in *Philadelphia, PA* and is now residing at *deceased*. . . . I was domiciled in the United States, my permanent residence being at *Narberth* in the State of *Pennsylvania*, where I follow the occupation of *Nursing*. My last passport was obtained from *Never had any*. . . . I am about to go abroad temporarily; and I intend to return to the United States within *1 years* with the purpose of working and performing the duties of citizenship therein; and I desire a passport for visiting the countries hereinafter named for the following purpose:

Turkey
Nursing—Red Cross   *Relief work*

OATH OF ALLEGIANCE:
Further, I do solemnly swear that I will support and defend the Constitution of the United States against all enemies, foreign and domestic; that I will bear true faith and allegiance to the same; and that I take this obligation freely, without any mental reservations or purpose of evasion: So help me God. *18 January, 1919*

F.2

Official listings for Alice Clark, Edith Cold, and Mary Super as they appear in Charles V. Vickrey, *Teamwork: A Tribute and an Appeal*

VOL. III	JUNE 13, 1924	No. 6

This tribute to returned overseas workers compiled eight lists, including those who had returned, overseas personnel, administrative committees, and returned faculty members from the American University at Beirut, the International College at Smyrna, Robert College in Constantinople, and the Constantinople Women's College. It concludes with a roster of the dead. Below, I have provided the opening remarks by Vickrey and the entries for Alice Clark, Edith Cold, and Mary Super.

VETERANS' NUMBER
A TRIBUTE AND AN APPEAL

Nearly a thousand men and women have served in connection with the overseas activities of Near East Relief. *Twenty-three of this number have died in the service.* Several of these clearly sacrificed their lives as a result of heroic volunteer service in posts of recognized danger. Others have been seriously maimed, have sacrificed limb, sight and health as a result of faithfulness in the performance of self-sacrificing service that transcended duty. Life, limb, sight, health, have gone without murmur or complaint. Facing their sacrifice, "It is rather for us to be here dedicated to the great task remaining before us—that from these honored dead we take increased devotion to that cause for which they gave the last full measure of devotion." As a result of the sacrifice of these lives, of the devoted service of the more than 700 returned workers who are now in America, and of the contributions of many millions of dollars from the American people, there are living today at least a million people who otherwise would have perished from deportation, exposure, starvation and disease. A disproportionately large number of those who have been saved are little children. Most of the children once in our orphanages have already been graduated or restored to self-support and useful industry. Approximately 50,000 of the younger and more dependent children are still in our institutions or in supervised homes.

To what purpose have these lives been saved? If we have merely kept alive a million human animals as possible cannon-fodder for some future war, the sacrifices mentioned above have been in vain and not worth the precious American lives laid down in the process of salvage. *The real test of our work is yet before us.* These children must be not merely so many lives saved but so many forces for righteousness, progress, world brotherhood and peace, permeating and transforming the industrial and social life of the Near East. To quit now is to sacrifice much of what has gone before and in large measure to invalidate the life sacrifices of our comrades. In their memory and for their sake as well as for the sake of the world's future we must carry on until these dependent children have become worthy heirs and exponents of the high idealism that led the thousand American men and women to offer themselves for outpost salvage service in the Near East.

VOLUNTEERS DESIRED FOR HOME SERVICE

The strength of Near East Relief has always been in the volunteer service and sacrificial spirit of its officers, committeemen and workers. The continuation of this spirit is now especially needed in the home field and we earnestly appeal to those returned workers who have given their term of honorable service in the Near East now to volunteer a continuation of that service in America. No others are as well qualified to help. You have seen the field. You have helped to save these thousands of children. You have witnessed the devotion of your associates in the service. You can tell the story as no one else can. On the platform, through the press, and especially through organization and leadership in committees, an indispensable service beyond valuation can be rendered. We appeal for such service as well as for any suggestions based upon past experience that may enable us to bring to a worthy consummation the splendid work which you helped to pioneer overseas, for which the American people have contributed generously and to which our fallen comrades have given their lives.

CHARLES V. VICKREY,
General Secretary, Near East Relief.

List I
Returned overseas workers with present occupations and addresses.

CLARK, ALICE K. (Miss), of Evanston, Illinois, went with the "Leviathan" party and taught at Hadjin. During the more than six months' siege of the town the American compound was captured by the Turks but the diplomacy of the Near East Relief people protected the 300 orphans from the attackers. For several days the Near East Relief personnel and several missionaries were forced to live in a closet under the stairs. When the Turks recaptured the buildings on June 13 the inmates were taken to a Turkish camp and held for two days before being sent on to Caesarea. Miss Cold and Miss Super shared these exciting experiences. Miss Clark left Constantinople for the U.S.A. July 10, 1920, and is now living at 1217 Forest Avenue, Evanston, Illinois.

COLD, EDITH (Miss), of Oberlin, Ohio, went out on February 16, 1919, and was appointed to Hadjin. With Miss Alice Clark and Miss Super she endured the siege of that town, being fired on by the Turks when she carried a white flag into the compound of the orphanage. With the others she made her way to Talas and on to Constantinople. From there she went to Beirut at the end of 1920 and then on to Adana where she was for a year in the American School for Girls. She was decorated by the French for her work for French prisoners. From Adana, she went to Marash. She is now doing missionary work in Aleppo. (June, 1924)

SUPER, MARY W. (Miss), of Narberth, Pa., another "Leviathan"-ite, had thrilling experiences during the siege of Hadjin. She had nursed a Turkish officer back to health and his intervention somewhat lessened the difficulties of the besieged. On June 13, 1920, the Turks captured the buildings and ordered out the Americans, allowing them to carry only hand baggage. On July 20, 1920, Miss Super left Constantinople, on her way to the States. She is now doing private nursing in Narberth, Pa., her address being 728 Montgomery Avenue.

F.3

Letters and telegrams sent by Alice Clark's father and brother to the State Department, the Secretary of State, and other government representatives seeking information on the safety of the relief workers near the end of the siege (June 16 – July 3, 1920)

TELEGRAM RECEIVED

FROM

Chicago, Ill.
June 16, 1920
Recd. 1.26 p.m.

State Department
    Washington D. C.

Can you locate and get word from my daughter Miss Alice K Clark, Near East Relief. Last word received direct from her was dated March sixth from Hadjin, Cilicia, Asia Minor.

GEORGE M CLARK

GEORGE M. CLARK & COMPANY

DIVISION AMERICAN STOVE COMPANY

GEORGE M. CLARK,
MANAGER
CABLE ADDRESS
"CLARK JEWEL" CHICAGO

Stoves CLARK JEWEL Ranges

179 NORTH MICHIGAN AVENUE

CHICAGO

NEW YORK
IRVIN W. PEFFLY, SALES AGENT
SAN FRANCISCO
B.S. PEDERSEN, SALES AGENT

June 16/'20

Hon. Lawrence Y. Sherman,
Springfield, Ill.

Dear Sir:—

Enclosed please find copy of telegram sent to the State Department this morning by my father.

My sister, Miss Alice K. Clark, at her own expense, joined the Near East Relief, and has been serving for a year in Hadjin, Cilicia, Asian Minor, and she was due to leave for home early in March. At Hadjin there were also a relief worker, Miss Mary Super of Narberth, Penn., and a missionary, Miss Edith Cold, of Cleveland, O.

The last word we have had direct from my sister was a letter dated March 6th.

Letters from friends in Adana and newspaper dispatches have advised that communication has been interrupted while Hadjin has been under siege by the Nationalists. The last report has it that some little time ago the mission compound was surrendered to the Nationalist, but that no word had come through as to the health or safety of the three American women.

I am writing to you hoping that you can see that every effort is made to get news from these three American women, and if possible their release.

You may be sure that my parents and myself will greatly appreciate anything you can have done towards this end.

Yours very truly,
ROBERT K. CLARK

RKC/HH

GEORGE M. CLARK & COMPANY

DIVISION AMERICAN STOVE COMPANY

GEORGE M. CLARK,
MANAGER
CABLE ADDRESS
"CLARK JEWEL" CHICAGO

Stoves CLARK JEWEL Ranges

179 NORTH, MICHIGAN AVENUE

CHICAGO

NEW YORK
IRVIN W. PEFFLY, SALES AGENT
SAN FRANCISCO
B.S. PEDERSEN, SALES AGENT

June 16/'20

State Department,
 Washington, D. C.

Dear Gentlemen:—

Enclosed please find confirmation of my wire today, asking you to get word if possible from my daughter, Miss Alice K. Clark.

Something over a year ago my daughter reached her station at Hadjin, Cilicia, and was due to come out the early part of this last March.

No direct word has come from her since a letter dated March 6th at Hadjin, and all we have learned since is from friends in Adana and from newspaper reports.

I will be pleased to receive any information you get of the three Americans that have been located at Hadjin, there being beside my daughter Miss Edith Cold of Cleveland, O. and Miss Mary Super of Narberth, Penn.

Yours very truly,
GEORGE M. CLARK

GMC/HH

THE YOUNG WOMEN'S CHRISTIAN ASSOCIATION OF CHICAGO

CENTRAL BRANCH

Phone Randolph 2420   59 E. Monroe Street

June 17, 1920

Honorable Bainbridge Colby,
Secretary of State,
Washington, D. C.

Sir:

We are very deeply distressed with the news that is now some four months old, that Miss Alice K. Clark, 1217 Forest Ave. Evanston, Ill. is being kept as a prisoner of war by the Nationalist party in Hadjin, Turkey. We understand that no word whatsoever has come from Hadjin since March and that many instances of perfidy on the part of the Turks have occurred there and in other parts of the country.

We are wondering what steps have been taken by our government to protect its citizens in this terrible land. Miss Cold and Miss Clark have been alone in this mountain city and although we hope they have been in reasonable safety we do feel that something very definite should be done by our government to make the Turks feel that a single citizen of America is as safe as a citizen of the British Empire. As a resident of Turkey myself during the massacres of and about 1896 we had abundant occasion to know what dignity the name of the British citizen carried with it and this is indeed well known throughout the civilized world.

The immediate concern with us is, however, a more personal one than the honor due to our own country. The women are alone, and unprotected. Their families and friends have borne a weight of anxiety that they should carry no longer. Cannot measures be taken for their safety and word sent to the parents who are almost in despair of this accomplished fact?

Very truly yours,
HARRIET A. LEE
Director of General Education.

Woman's Board of Missions of the Interior
(CONGREGATIONAL)
19 SOUTH LA SALLE STREET, ROOM 1315
TELEPHONE CENTRAL 1388
CABLE ADDRESS "WOBODIN, CHICAGO"
CHICAGO

June 17, 1920

State Department,
Washington, D. C.

Gentlemen:—

I write today to urge you to use every possible means to secure information relative to the condition of the three American women now held as prisoners by the Nationalistic Turkish forces in Hadjin, Cilicia. These three women are — Miss Edith Cold, Cleveland; Miss Alice K. Clark, Evanston, Illinois, and Miss Mary Super, Narbeth, Pennsylvania. The two former are close personal friends.

We understand that they surrendered under the white flag in April and we have been unable to get word from them since. We depend upon you to get in touch with them and to use every possible means to secure their release and return to America.

Respectfully yours,

EULA B. LEE
(Mrs. Lucius O. Lee)

TELEGRAM SENT

𝔇epartment of 𝔖tate,
Washington

June 18, 1920.

George M. Clark
  Chicago, Illinois.

Ordinary communication between the United States and Hadjin closed. Department endeavoring other channels ascertain welfare Americans that city. You will be advised upon receipt information concerning your daughter. Suggested you also communicate Near East Relief, 1 Madison Avenue, New York City.

                        BAINBRIDGE COLBY
                        Secretary of State.

367.1115 C54/—
Co DDS.EHR

POSTAL TELEGRAPH – COMMERCIAL CABLES
CLARENCE H. MACKAY, PRESIDENT

TELEGRAM

COPY

120CHB 1234P 13 GOVT

CONSTANTINOPLE JUNE 30

CLARK JEWEL

(GEO M CLARK CO 179 N MICH CHGO)

FOLLOWING FROM SAMSOON

QUOTE *SAFE WELL ALICE* UNQUOTE 10429

STANV

GEORGE M. CLARK & COMPANY
DIVISION AMERICAN STOVE COMPANY

GEORGE M. CLARK, MANAGER
CABLE ADDRESS
"CLARK JEWEL" CHICAGO

Stoves CLARK JEWEL Ranges

179 NORTH, MICHIGAN AVENUE
CHICAGO

NEW YORK
IRVIN W. PEFFLY, SALES AGENT
SAN FRANCISCO
B.S. PEDERSEN, SALES AGENT

July 2, 1920

The Secretary of State,
   Washington, D. C.

Dear Sir:—

Your letter of June 29th is received while my father is in Boston.

Yesterday when I returned from New York I found that a cable had been received the day before, copy of which is enclosed.

We are wondering if the signature is an American Consular Agent in Constantinople.

We, of course, would like to know whether my sister is still in the interior and the message that she is "Safe and Well" was relayed through Samsoon, or whether she is there.

Of course, if she is there we would like to know what the chance is of her being transferred to Constantinople, from which point she, of course, could readily leave for home.

We certainly hope that you can get further information in regard to her location and arrange for her transport to Constantinople if she is now in Samsoon.

Very truly yours,
ROBERT K. CLARK

RKO:S

TELEGRAM SENT

𝕯epartment of 𝕾tate,
Washington

July 2, 1920.

Near East Relief,
  One Madison Avenue,
    New York City

Department has received following telegram dated July 1st from high Commissioner Constantinople:

Quote
News from Hadjin until thirteenth June. Armenians still hold Hadjin. Mary Super, Catherine Bredemus [sic] *and Alice Clark, have arrived Samsoun, and proceeding Constantinople. Edith Cole* [sic]*, well. This accounts for all Americans who were in Hadjin.*
Unquote.

NORMAN DAVIS
ACTING SECRETARY OF STATE

367.116/751
AKS/MNB

NE

TELEGRAM SENT

Department of State,
Washington

July 3, 1920.

Mr. George M. Clark
  179 North Michigan Avenue,
    Chicago, Illinois.

Reference your telegram June sixteen. American Commissioner Constantinople reports Mary Super and Alice Clark have reached Samsoun and proceeding to Constantinople. Edith Cold well.

A. A. ADEE
ACTING SECRETARY OF STATE

NPD/MMP
CO—367.1115C54/3

F.4

Mary Super's Obituary,
Main Line Chronicle, Ardmore, PA, July 22, 1965

DEATHS

MISS MARY W. SUPER

Mary W. Super, 83, last of the children of Jacob Super, died on July 14 and was buried in St. Paul's Cemetery following services conducted Saturday morning by the Rev. Donal Doll, pastor of St. Paul's Lutheran Church, Ardmore.

The Super family lived in the family home at 1256 Montgomery Ave., Narberth, for the past century. On the property still stands the old blacksmith and wheelwright building which did a flourishing business during the last century when the group of houses, most of them still standing, formed the village of Libertyville. It was one of the stops on the old Columbia Railroad.

In the rear of the Super homestead, which was built in the 1840's, is Indian Springs, the source of the main branch of Indian Springs Creek, where the Swedes are said to have had a trading post before William Penn's time.

Miss Super, a practical nurse, was born in the family home. She was known for her helpfulness to others.

She is survived by two nieces, Miss Charlotte Super and Mrs. Joseph Hunter.

SOURCES AND SELECTED BIBLIOGRAPHY

The Armenian Genocide and America's Outcry: A Compilation of U.S. Documents 1890-1923. Washington D.C.: Armenian Assembly of America, 1985.

Aydin, Mustafa, and Cagri Erhan, eds. *Turkish-American Relations: Past, Present, and Future*. London: Routledge, 2004.

Bamyeh, Mohammed, "Global Order and the Historical Structures of Dar al-Islam," in Manfred B. Steger, ed., *Rethinking Globalism*. Lanham, MD: Rowman and Littlefield, 2004.

Barton, James Levy. *The Story of Near East Relief (1915-1930): An Interpretation*. New York: Macmillan, 1930.

Bierstadt, Edward Hale. *The Great Betrayal; A Survey of the Near Eastern Problem*. New York: Robert M. McBride and Co., 1924. [Also published in London by Hutchinson and Co., 1924.]

Clark, Alice Keep. *Letters from Cilicia*. Chicago: A. D. Weinthrop & Co., 1924.

Dadrian, Vahakn N. *The History of the Armenian Genocide: Ethnic Conflict from the Balkans to Anatolia to the Caucasus*, 6th rev. ed. New York and Oxford: Berghahn Books, 2003. Originally published in 1995.

Eby, Blanche Remington. *At the Mercy of Turkish Brigands: A True Story*. New Carlisle, Ohio: Bethel Publishing Co., 1922.

Grabill, Joseph L. *Protestant Diplomacy and the Near East: Missionary Influence on American Policy, 1810-1927*. Minneapolis: University of Minnesota Press, 1971.

Hovannisian, Richard G., ed. *The Armenian Republic: The First Year, 1918-1919*. Vol. 1. Los Angeles: University of California Press, 1971.

———. *The Armenian Genocide: History, Politics, Ethics*. New York and Hampshire, England: Palgrave Macmillan, 1992.

Katchadourian, Stina, ed. *Great Need over the Water: The Letters of Theresa Huntington Ziegler, Missionary to Turkey, 1898-1905*. Ann

Arbor: The Gomidas Institute/Taderon Press: 1999.

Kazanjian, Paren. *The Cilician Armenian Ordeal*. Boston: Hye Intentions, Inc., 1989.

Kerr, Stanley Elphinstone. *The Lions of Marash: Personal Experiences with American Near East Relief, 1919-1922*. New York: State University of New York, 1973.

Lambert, Rose. *Hadjin and the Armenian Massacres*. New York: Fleming H. Revell Company, 1911.

Miller, Donald E., and Lorna Touryan Miller. *Survivors: An Oral History of the Armenian Genocide*. Berkeley and Los Angeles: University of California Press, 1993.

Nalbandian, Louise. *The Armenian Revolutionary Movement: The Development of Armenian Political Parties through the Nineteenth Century*. Berkeley and Los Angeles: University of California Press, 1963.

Ross, Frank A. *The Near East and American Philanthropy; A Survey Conducted under the Guidance of the General of the Near East Survey*. New York: Columbia University Press, 1929.

Vickrey, Charles V. *Teamwork: A Tribute and an Appeal*, ed. Mabell S. C. Smith. New York: Near East Relief National Headquarters Publication, 1924.

Zürcher, Erik J. *Turkey: A Modern History*. London and New York: I. B. Tauris & Co. Ltd., 1993.